For my boy Myron.

CULTURE SHOCK!

Switzerland

Shirley Eu-Wong

Graphic Arts Center Publishing Company
Portland, Oregon

In the same series

Argentina	*France*	*Malaysia*	*Sweden*
Australia	*Germany*	*Mauritius*	*Switzerland*
Bolivia	*Greece*	*Mexico*	*Syria*
Borneo	*Hong Kong*	*Morocco*	*Taiwan*
Britain	*Hungary*	*Myanmar*	*Thailand*
Burma	*India*	*Nepal*	*Turkey*
California	*Indonesia*	*Netherlands*	*UAE*
Canada	*Iran*	*Norway*	*Ukraine*
Chile	*Ireland*	*Pakistan*	*USA*
China	*Israel*	*Philippines*	*USA—The South*
Cuba	*Italy*	*Singapore*	*Venezuela*
Czech Republic	*Japan*	*South Africa*	*Vietnam*
Denmark	*Korea*	*Spain*	
Egypt	*Laos*	*Sri Lanka*	

Barcelona At Your Door	*Paris At Your Door*	*Living and Working*
Chicago At Your Door	*Rome At Your Door*	*Abroad*
Havana At Your Door		*Working Holidays*
Jakarta At Your Door	*A Globe-Trotter's Guide*	*Abroad*
Kuala Lumpur, Malaysia	*A Parent's Guide*	
At Your Door	*A Student's Guide*	
London At Your Door	*A Traveller's Medical Guide*	
New York At Your Door	*A Wife's Guide*	

Illustrations by Shirley Eu-Wong
Photographs from Shirley Eu-Wong and Charles Eu

© 1996 Times Editions Pte Ltd
© 2000 Times Media Private Limited
Revised 1999
Reprinted 1997, 1998, 2001

This book is published by special
arrangement with Times Media Private Limited
Times Centre, 1 New Industrial Road, Singapore 536196
International Standard Book Number 1-55868-248-1
Library of Congress Catalog Number 95-79456
Graphic Arts Center Publishing Company
P.O. Box 10306 • Portland, Oregon 97296-0306 • (503) 226-2402

Printed in Singapore

CONTENTS

Preface 7

1 The Switzer-land of Flowing Milk and Money 9
2 Confederation Helvetia 15
3 The Facts of Life 34
4 Folklore Galore and Entertainment Today 55
5 Ski, Surf, Sun and Skincare 68
6 Education: Public, Private and the Very Private 79
7 Do's, Don'ts and Dunnos 89
8 One-day Excursions to Somewhere Else 104
9 From Aargau Carrot Cake to Zurich Sliced Veal 113
10 All About Business 127
11 Last Resorts and Last Remarks 139

Cultural Quiz 147
Glossary 158
Bibliography 160
Acknowledgements 162
The Author 163
Index 164

PREFACE

Once upon three years ago, I left Switzerland five months pregnant and with a heart as heavy as a wheel of Swiss Emmenthal riding in the tote bag full of salami and Valais wine. Everything about Switzerland had enriched my life, from eating to socialising to the onerous tasks of cleaning and cooking. "When in Rome, do as the Romans do" is a wise saying. When we approach it with an open mind, we might even find improvements. Going back to the country where the people's habits are as meticulous as the way they write their numbers, I've rediscovered a newness that comes from a country that is now more open to changes with the introduction of the Euro dollar and the slow lifting of recession and unemployment.

I revisited the country during the worst snowstorms of the century. But true to form, the trains continued to run, the roads snowploughed, and it's business *comme d'habitude*. So much about Switzerland is about its natural beauty that even in the seemingly unpleasant climate (I might add dangerous), there is much to admire.

The cost of living in Switzerland printed in this book is correct at the time of printing, but even as the world turns, prices keep escalating. Most foreign expressions are in French, so if you need the German or Italian versions, refer to the Glossary at the end of the book. A fair bit of material was based on personal experience, hence many of the unfortunate incidents were a direct product of our naïveté – which is to say, it may not happen to you in exactly the same way, but there is a tendency for recurrence if you do not take our folly into consideration. With the Internet shrinking the world and the Euro currency being introduced, there's a fair bit more to Switzerland than what meets your eyes.

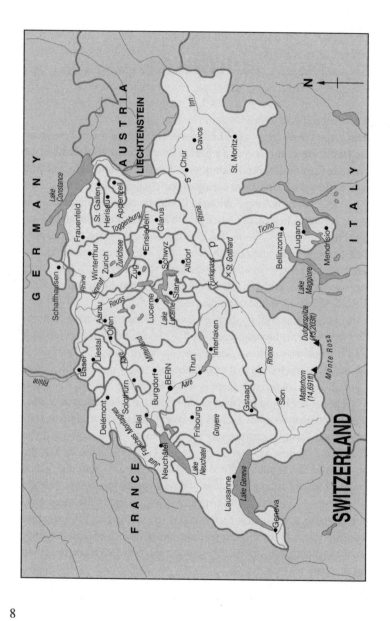

GERMANY

AUSTRIA

LIECHTENSTEIN

Lake Constance

Schaffhausen

Frauenfeld

St. Gallen
Herisau
Appenzell
Toggenburg

Winterthur
Zurich
Linmat
Zurichsee

Einsiedeln

Glarus

Chur

Inn

Davos

St. Moritz

Rhine

Schwyz

Altdorf

Zug

Reuss

Aarau

Olten

Liestal

Basel

Aare

Rhine

Mittelland

Lucerne

Lake Lucerne

Stans

Furkapass

× St. Gotthard

Ticino

Bellinzona

Lugano

Mendrisio

Lake Maggiore

ITALY

Burgdorf

BERN

Aare

Thun

Interlaken

Rhone

Dufourspitze
(15,203ft)

Monte Rosa

Solothurn

Montagnes

Delémont

Biel

Jura

Fribourg

Gruyere

Gstaad

Sion

Matterhorn
(14,691ft)

FRANCE

Neuchâtel

Lake Neuchâtel

Lausanne

Lake Geneva

Geneva

SWITZERLAND

N

Rhine

— *Chapter One* —

THE SWITZER-LAND OF FLOWING MILK AND MONEY

To say that Switzerland is all cows and mountains is rather like biting into a delicious foot-long French eclair without the double cream inside. Certainly it is done; however, it would cause Jean-Pierre, our pâtissier, a great deal of distress that the best parts have been overlooked. Coming to Switzerland in the full-blown Alpine chill on a frosty December morning in 1991 (on a double cream-free diet), the husband and I were to discover that the best view of Switzerland is the one from below.

Circling some 3,000 metres up in the Jura mountains amid fluffy clouds, we imagined the copiousness of the land, snowcapped mountains, numerous flumes snaking through timeworn boondocks and hillocks in leafy wooded greens – in short, a picture pretty much like the travelogue's much hyped, much painted and photographed version of idyllic life in Old Swissland. All that we had heard, heard regaled about, and herded like cattle to believe, is that Switzerland is cows, chocolates and cheese. In due time, as we settled in, the curative effect of whitewashing prior clichés gradually began. In their place settled a more sombre reality that we had just landed in one of the world's wealthiest, most exclusive and private country clubs, which also happens *to be* a country.

The Swiss Embassy back home hardly prepared us for any culture shock; perhaps believing strongly that Singapore's similar governing methods must indeed be Swiss-inspired. They could have told us to replace any urbanised illusions of twenty-four hour night activities with village serenity and vast amounts of consideration from neighbours. This invariably includes us unless we were to rent or purchase our own château on our own little hill, surrounded by our own little acreage of pines and firs. Tough chance. In other words, the after effects of coming to Switzerland would register high on the Culture Shock scale.

Enfin, as the Suisses Romands (the kosher way of calling the Swiss-French) would say, we arrived in apple-pie order Geneva. We had survived the awesome view from our precious window seat, murmuring "Uoohh", and "Woaahhhh!" for about 20 minutes. Switzerland was looking more modern than mythical, more business than plain busy. It looked affluent too, but never beyond being self-sufficient. Its business is always dealing with other people. It is unlike many other European countries, and perhaps within its confederacy, that is neither good nor bad. Neutrality is frugality, or so some say. Be that as it may, the Swiss Confederation had been neutral enough to let us in peaceably as in the past it let in other foreigners like Lord Byron, Leon Gambetta, Igor Stravinsky, Jean Calvin, Vladimir Nabokov and Charles Chaplin – among other dignitaries too royal to mention.

Someone had kindly warned us (could well be someone from the Swiss Embassy) before we left our land – Getting in is the easy part, it's *staying in* that's difficult. So, a word of caution to all tireless travellers waiting to savour the fat of Switzerland. Double cream is tasty, but its effect may forever change the way you look at an eclair again.

ARRIVING IN THE CLINIC OF THE WORLD

So there we were in the centre of Europe, in one of the world's most international airports – so international, you can hardly pick out the locals. Bevies of travellers speaking four languages and a dialect are the constant sounds in Switzerland's airport lounges. As we waited for our luggage of thermals and woollies to come tumbling onto the conveyor belt, the stark contrast of reality versus the last ten minutes of delusions hit our most tangible senses. Whether alone, with your spouse, or with your entire brood of children and family pets, your immediate, almost infuriating desire is to talk at once. Now that you have finally reached Geneva, city of Calvinists and expensive boutiques, the topic of your discussion will invariably be, *where to first?* In spite of earlier complaints of queasiness, ear popping, or irritating air pockets, merely arriving in Switzerland will become the panacea to all sufferers of travel-related sickness. All one has to do is stroll out of the airport into the invigorating alpine fresh air.

The Swiss authorities are a kindly sort who can be just as eager to let you through as you are eager to go through. However, do not by any means attempt to 1) smuggle drugs, 2) smuggle illegal weapons, or 3) do anything listed on the disembarkation card as being offensive or criminal. This is because their laws are stringent, effective, and very often carried out swiftly and painfully. For the alluded criminal in question, undoubtedly.

If you have to arrive at your final destination by train, taxi or car, you will not get a medal for asking for directions at the information desk, but you will feel relieved if you did. Languages are a speciality in Switzerland. Most Swiss are trilingual, and often have very good gestures and face twitches that will answer your most banal queries.

HAVE CAR WILL TRAVEL

Hertz and Budget are known the world over as car rental companies, so if you prefer to drive yourself around, rent yourself a car. You should be able to leave it at the next destination office, but remember that an extra charge will be included. Insurance coverage is compulsory and details of payments and how to return the vehicle will be explained. Enquire about road maps and weather conditions if you have to scale a snowy mountain top to get to your destination. This is vitally important if you are not used to driving in such conditions. (More details about driving and transportation are given in Chapter Three.)

GET ME TO THE TRAIN ON TIME

Swiss trains are well-and-world-renowned to be punctual to the minute. They have built a reputation for themselves to be the most reliable form of rail transport this side of the Milky Way. The trains can be found in the lower levels of both Zurich and Geneva airports. We were delighted to find the ticket office (French: *guichet*, German: *Fahrkartenschalter*) in a strategically and logically located spot. Ticket vending machines are also quite convenient, and you will probably single out the locals from the foreigners by the deft way they slide the notes into the right slot in the machine.

Ask for special reduced rates if you are under 26 or above 55. Young children or infants can also travel for less than the normal fare. The half-price fare called the *demi-tarif* is extremely useful but will cost you about Sfr. 150 per person, and is valid for a year.

The key to enjoying the benefits of the country's excellent transportation is to step forward and ask. Clarify if the fare is for one way, or includes the return trip. Train tickets are usually valid for a day. You may want to enquire about special passes which include transportation by rail, by ferry and by yellow Post buses. Transportation is assuredly expensive and unless you are thinking of purchasing some wheels of your own, a year-long pass will invariably save you the most. The Swiss Pass (unlimited travel throughout Switzerland for periods of 4 days to a month) or the Swiss Card (transportation to and from your destination plus 50% off excursions) are mostly for tourists and can be purchased at all major railway stations.

Obtain your ticket before you get on, and do not attempt any wheeling or dealing with the conductor who incidentally reminds you of your third grade teacher of whom you lived in terror. Anything short of the exact fare is subject to a fine. And when they hand you a ticket for the fine, they do mean for you to pay up on the spot.

HAIL ME A MERCEDES...

The Mercedes, Volvos and VWs are taxis. If they have a yellow coloured box on their roof, you can go ahead and get a smooth ride to your destination. You will be curious to find that rows of shining new luxury cars are lining up outside awaiting your fare, but after a short ride, you will be bowled over at the rate they charge and will wonder no more why more people don't take cabs.

This is the clinic of the world, hailed by world-class travellers as the pinnacle of morals and cleanliness, health and well-being. The first encounter with Switzerland might knock the wind out of you, as it certainly did us, but it promises not to leave you maladjusted to the ways of the Swiss.

Slowly, but surely, the mountainscape and the placid lakes will ease the uneasiness of your being there. Sooner or later, we succumbed to the sweet-doing-nothing pace of living there and got the feeling we didn't want to be anywhere else.

Chapter Two

CONFEDERATION HELVETIA

Many have often chanced to remark what a curious country Switzerland is, perhaps much less a country than an extension of its neighbours. It is almost as if someone had cordoned off the outer extremes of Germany, France, Italy and Austria to magically produce the Swiss Confederation. The dotted line is firmly drawn on the map and *voilà* – instant Switzerland! The truth, however, cannot be farther from such naive reasoning, and has more historical ramifications than the conquests of Pope Innocent IV.

HISTORY OF THE OATH OF GRÜTLI

In the early 13th century, under the watchful eyes of the Holy Roman Empire, three southwestern German-speaking towns were granted autonomous government within their regions of Uri, Schwyz, and Unterwalden. As they prospered through successful trading with Germany and Italy, they decided to renew their earlier alliance to one another in August 1291. This did not guarantee immediate independence as it would take more than another 350 years before Switzerland legally became a sovereign and independent state in 1648. Although the surviving treaty between the three towns was discovered in Schwyz in 1760, legend has it that it was on the meadow of Rütli (also known as Grütli) that three representatives of Uri, Schwyz and Unterwalden had taken an oath of mutual allegiance, commonly known as *Eidgenossenschaft*, or the Society of the Oath.

The newborn Swiss Confederation had to weather peasant revolts, civil wars, religious wars, French invasion, liberal revolutions, conflicts between liberals and Catholic conservatives and numerous false starts in industrialising and revising its constitution. All this was before Switzerland came to be recognised as the pinnacle of racial tolerance, economic prowess and self-preserving neutrality. It became the country that had everything and owed nothing.

The 23 cantons (26, if one includes half-cantons) which make up Switzerland did not unify until as late as 1979, when Jura opted to separate from the parent canton of Bern to stand independently. From depending on one another to ensure prolonged prosperity to becoming 26 independent cantons striving to support a multiracial confederation, Switzerland had transformed itself from a treaty of three to a peaceful country of plenty. Perhaps the most ingenious part of the nation's history lies in its continual efforts to centralise the constitution, despite differences threatening to overturn these efforts. By the 19th century, 1 August 1291 formally became the Swiss National Day – a day that celebrates the founding of the Swiss Confederation and the Society of the Oath. It is on this day that many come to understand

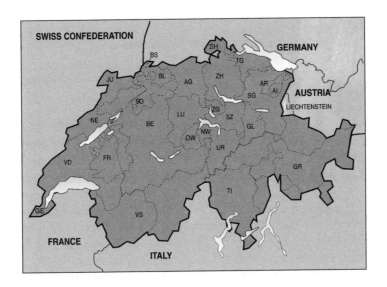

that Switzerland's crucial beginnings were humble ones, relying on the mutual trust of three men, and their loyalty and co-dependence on one another to nurture the basic parameters of their contract.

The 26 cantons (see map above) are:

AG	Aargau	NW	Nidwalden
AI	Appenzell (Inner-Rhodes)	OW	Obwalden
AR	Appenzell (Outer-Rhodes)	SG	St. Gallen
BE	Bern	SH	Schaffhausen
BL	Basel-country	SO	Solothurn
BS	Basel-town	SZ	Schwyz
FR	Fribourg	TG	Thurgau
GE	Geneva	TI	Ticino
GL	Glarus	UR	Uri
GR	Grisons	VD	Vaud
JU	Jura	VS	Valais
LU	Lucerne	ZG	Zug
NE	Neuchâtel	ZH	Zurich

LANGUAGE

"You taught me the language; and my profit on't
Is, I know how to curse."

—William Shakespeare, *The Tempest*

Foreign gibberish. An unintelligible blabbering which sounds so lilting yet profound that for a minute I was mesmerised by their conversation. It consisted of long and short words, contused by sharp emphasis at the end of remarks, very often ending like a reprimand from an acute professor. The two expensive-looking *mesdames* were very likely enjoying a little tête-à-tête in a small cafe, yet I could not help but imagine the one in the fur coat making an insidious comment on the sorry state of my unpressed pants. If only I had been more insightful and memorised the few unkind words from my French tutor, I would surely know if I should be indignant or indifferent.

The greatest unspoken fear while in a foreign country must be the feeling of utter helplessness. In Switzerland, the chance of misunderstanding occurring is greater than snowfall in the mountains. There are four national languages in Switzerland, and that is enough to render even the locals foreign in their own country. It is not surprising that, as true foreigners, you and I might come face to face with several awkward situations.

In terms of frequency of use, the Swiss-German language, or more accurately, Schwyzerdütsch, takes the lead, being the predominant language in 72% of the country (central and northeastern), while French parleys in 33% (western). Italian is heard a lot in 14.5% (southern) and the peasant dialect of Rhaeto-Romansch is being kept alive in about 0.9% (southeastern). English is finding itself into schools this October 1999 and is spoken by 10.9% of foreigners living in Switzerland. Logical deduction puts the remaining 11.2% as a mysterious mixture of patois from neighbouring countries. The Swiss are fluent in at least two languages.

The wide variety of languages need not be viewed as some communication obstacle that you are expected to vault over effort-

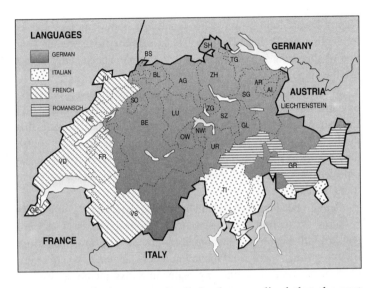

lessly. Through the years, the Swiss have realised that the vast majority of the world speaks (or at least understands) English. It is therefore now quite common to find Swiss university students trilingual and very glib in English. No doubt there will still be moments when you feel at a loss, not comprehending their deliberately sloweddown palaver; it is imperative that you give yourself a chance to learn through careful watching and listening. Frustration is only overcome by determination and patience, my tutor used to say.

Language is not merely used to communicate; one employs it to flatter, charm or please in order to get something from someone. When you fork out some Sfr. 350 for language classes, don't be taken aback by the manner in which the professor teaches. You will learn the language as a child might learn the etiquette of dining with the queen – formally and with a deep sense of dignity.

When my Taiwanese friend enters the supermarket, it often astounds me the number of sales people she knows. Never one to shy away from monosyllabic French, and with a disposition that makes

Happy Dwarf look grumpy, her facial and body language speaks louder than her French. The lesson here is this: try to overcome your fear of appearing foolish, throw yourself into the deep end, and just use the language.

Where you live will greatly determine which language you speak, or learn to speak. In larger or simply more touristy cities, you will find English spoken at its best. In smaller towns or villages, it is natural that the local language is the only means of communicating. Of course they can insist that you, being the foreigner, ought to at least make repeated attempts to speak their tongue; after all, you decided to move to their locale.

Perhaps because Switzerland boasts four languages, you will not be surprised to find language schools as prevalent as cows on a country hill. If you are undaunted by any adverse prospects from investing time, energy and money in a new language, you are very likely to succeed in integrating better in Swiss society as well as earning some respect from locals and Europeans alike.

Many language books are to be found in bookshops, and even the ubiquitous newsstands carry basic paperback translators such as Berlitz for the helpless foreigner. Below is a list, which although elementary, will help you recognise some of the most commonly used words and phrases in the three most common languages in Switzerland. It should help you get across at least a simple message. You won't get a standing ovation for trying out your pidgin French, your crooked German or your less than effusive Italian, but you might experience waves of warm appreciation from the Swiss, which could be incentive enough for you to jump on the language bandwagon to bilingualism. *Maybe* even trilingualism.

Social Niceties (French / German / Italian)

Good morning / Bonjour / Guten Morgen / Buon giorno
Good evening / Bonsoir / Guten Tag / Buona sera
Goodnight / Bonne nuit / Gute Nacht / Buona notte

My name is / Je m'appelle / Ich heisse / Mi chiamo

How are you? / Comment allez-vous? / Wie geht es Ihnen? / Come sta?

How are things? / Comment ça va? / Wie geht's? / Come va?

Do you speak English? / Parlez-vous anglais? / Sprechen Sie Englisch? / Parla inglese?

Do you understand? / Comprenez-vous? / Verstehen Sie? / Capisce?

How do you say that in French (German, Italian)? / Comment dit-on cela en français? / Wie heisst das auf deutsch? / Come si chiama questo in italiano?

Thank you / Merci / Danke / Grazie

You're welcome / Je vous en prie / Bitte / Prego

Don't mention it / Pas de quoi / Gern geschehen / Di niente

Sorry / Pardon / Es tut mir leid / Mi perdoni

Please / S'il vous plaît / Bitte / Per piacere, per favore

Excuse me / Excusez-moi / Verzeihung / Mi scusi

I don't know / Je ne sais pas / Ich weiss nicht / Non so

With pleasure / Avec plaisir / Mit Vernügen / Con piacere

Just a second / Un moment / Augenblick mal / Un momento

What does that mean? / Que veut dire cela? / Was bedeutet das? / Che cosa significa?

Recognising the Shops

Bakery / Boulangerie / Bäckerei / fornaio

Barber shop / Coiffeur / Friseur / Barberia

Beauty parlour / un salon de beauté / ein Damensalon / una parrucchiera

Bookstore / une librairie / eine Buchhandlung / una libreria

Butcher / une boucherie / einen Fleischerladen / una macelleria

Camera shop / un magasin d'appareils-photo / ein Photogeschäft / un negozio de fotocine

Candy store / une confiserie / ein Süsswarenladen / un sale e tabacchi

Clothing store / un magasin de vêtements / ein Bekleidungsgeschäft / un negozio di abbigliamento

Delicatessen / une charcuterie / ein Delikatessengeschäft / una salumeria

Department store / un grand magasin / ein Warenhaus / i grandi magazzini

Pharmacy / une pharmacie / eine Apotheke / una farmacia

Dry cleaner / une teinturerie / eine chemische Reinigung / la tintoria

Florist / un fleuriste / ein Blumengeschäft / un fioraio

Gift shop / un magasin de souvenirs / ein Souvenirgeschäft / un negozio di regali

Hardware store / une quincaillerie / eine Eisenwarenhandlung / un negozio di ferramenta

Launderer / une blanchisserie / eine Wäscherei / lavanderia

Liquor store / un magasin de vins et spiritueux / eine Spirituosen-handlung / una enoteca

Newsstand / un kiosque à journaux / ein Zeitungsstand / un'edicola

Record store / un magasin de disques / ein Schallplattengeschäft / un negozio di dischi

Supermarket / un supermarché / ein Supermarkt / un supermercato

Tobacco shop / un bureau de tabac / ein Tabakladen / una tabaccheria

Toy store / un magasin de jouets / ein Spielwarengeschäft / un negozio di giocattoli

Wine merchant / un négociant en vins / eine Weinhandlung / una mescita

Important Signs

Do not enter / Défense d'entrer / Kein Zutritt / Divieto di transito

Danger / Danger / Gefahr / Pericolo

No smoking / Défense de fumer / Rauchen verboten / Vietato fumare

Forbidden / Interdit / Verboten / Vietato

One-way street / Sens unique / Einbahnstrasse / Senso unico

Pedestrian zone / Piétons / Fussgänger / Pedoni

Occupied / Occupé / Besetzt / Occupato

Vacant / Libre / Frei / Libero

Open / Ouvert / Offen / Aperto

Closed / Fermé / Geschlossen / Chiuso

Men's room / Hommes / Herrentoilette / Signore

Women's room / Dames / Damentoilette / Signora

Entrance / Entrée / Eingang / Entrata

Exit / Sortie / Ausgang / Uscita

Road closed / Barré / Gesperrt / Sbarrato

Pull / Tirez / Ziehen / Tirare

Push / Poussez / Drücken / Spingere

Do not touch / Ne pas toucher / Nicht berühren / Non toccare

Keep off the grass / Defénse de marcher sur l'herbe / Betreten des
  Rasens verboten / Non calpestare le aiuole

Elevator / Ascenseur / Aufzug / Ascensore

Hot / Chaud / Heiss / Caldo

Cold / Froid / Kalt / Freddo

Reserved / Réservé / Reserviert / Riservato

Timetable / Horaire / Fahrplan / Orario

Railway station / Gare / Bahnhof / Stazione

Customs / Douane / Zoll / Dogana

Cantonal Differences: What It Means To You

Even though the Swiss constitution was modelled on that of the United States, each of Switzerland's self-governing cantons reflects an enterprise that is obviously Swiss. Orderliness, tolerance of neighbours and acceptance of local government lie at the foundation of each cantonal republic's state of peace and prosperity. Cantonal heads control legislation, taxation, immigration and local affairs within their boundaries. From granting educational bursaries to ruling over welfare wages, each canton has its own way of dealing with the people who settle within its borders.

The basic requirements for foreigners vary little from canton to canton. Unless you are a tourist, you are expected to go to the controller of foreigners (which is where you obtain your authorisation to stay) to inform them of the length of your stay, its purpose, and by what means you intend to support yourself while in Switzerland. If you have been hired by a Swiss company, the exhaustive paperwork for your entire stay in Switzerland is likely to be handled by the personnel manager of that company.

If you are entering Switzerland with hopes of studying in one of their many fine private colleges or institutions, you will need a certificate from your school to testify to your student status for the number of years of study required by your diploma or degree course. It is often a good idea to check with the school or with the Swiss Embassy prior to your leaving your home country. I have heard of several cases of Switzerland-bound students being bundled back home because they could not afford full-time student status.

An 'A' permit (*Saisonbewilligung*) is a seasonal permit allowing nine months' residency within Switzerland. The remaining three months have to be spent abroad. Such a permit is normally granted to foreign workers, especially in the hotel industry or construction sector, on a short-term basis. After four years of successful reapplication the *saisonnier* can apply to live and work on a yearly basis.

A 'B' permit (*Aufenthaltsbewilligung*) is a yearly permit. It is most often granted to students and carries with it a restricted number of working privileges. A maximum of 15 working hours per week is allowed to full-time students.

A 'C' (also called an *Aufenthaltsbewilligung*) permit is equivalent to permanent residency or the green card. It grants the holder rights to working privileges similar to the native-born. To obtain a 'C' permit, you must stay in Switzerland for no less than 10 years. Even if you do marry a Swiss, you have to stay married in Switzerland for at least 5 years in order to be considered Swiss.

Your first brush with the department of immigration in your commune (the smallest administrative structure of the canton, called *Gemeinde* in German) will further help you understand the ways and workings of the canton in which you live. Because of the increasing number of illegal refugees living in Switzerland, communal administrations have tightened security and begun limiting the numbers of 'A' and 'B' permits. Now practically nonexistent, permanent residency and rights to working privileges are reserved for the select few who can make an economic difference in Switzerland.

Taxes, legislative laws and mandatory insurance affect Swiss and foreigners alike. As students living in the canton of Vaud, we have found many disadvantages owing to strict taxation and outrageous deposits for the telephone, electricity, television, radio, and of course the apartment. In our circle of friends, we have uncovered nastier taxation laws in the next commune, merely 7 kilometres away. Property taxes, road taxes, compulsory insurance for the home, car, and health are things to deal with rather than to avoid. There are many laws you will not be able to stand clear from.

In any case, *necede malis* – yield not to misfortune. The grass *is* greener in Switzerland, for they have manicured it every day for the past seven centuries. As the old adage goes – no pain, no gain.

ECONOMY

In a country that is both blessed and cursed by its extraordinarily mountainous terrain, Switzerland's economy was forced to take an industrial-commercial turn since relying on minerals and other raw materials would mean certain death. Primarily a small industrial country (compared to gargantuan France and Germany), Switzerland has managed to remain on the ladder of estimable success largely because of its dedication to the quality of its products.

Huge chemical and pharmaceutical factories flank industrialised roads outside the great city suburbs. Nothing to shout about really, considering chemical and physical science came into its own in Switzerland in the early 16th century; of note are the exploits of Theophrastus Bombastus von Hohenheim Paracelsus (1493–1541). Pharmacies litter the main avenues of large and small towns today, each pharmacy with a list of curative paracetamols as long as the good chemist's name. Everyday household brands such as Sandoz and Roche stand out pensively as flagships of proficiency and profitability.

Building and construction, tunnelling and excavating, hydro-geology and railroad planning contribute much to the Swiss GNP. Ten years ago, these sectors accounted for 15%, making them a prominent factor in the Swiss economy. With 30,000 million Swiss francs being spent annually on public and private building invest-ments, companies such as Basler & Hofmann (Zurich) and Interplan 4 SA (Lucerne) have gained international recognition as contractors that have made their presence felt abroad. Some of the most important capabilities of Swiss companies in the building sector made available worldwide include the assessment of technical and political risks, providing site supervisors and specialists, organising the procure-ment and transportation of building materials, and procuring or leasing construction equipment.

One of the prime reasons Switzerland excels in this field is because the Swiss have had many years of experience. The country's difficult topography demands ingenious planning and construction for roads and railways, with a view to preserving the panoramic beauty of its landscape. Many contractors can lay an asphalt road across a desert plain, but as soon as it starts to get hilly, it pays to call in a Swiss firm. Who better to suspend a bridge across the bay area than Swiss architect Othmar Ammann? His Golden Gate Bridge in San Francisco has gone down in the annals of bridge-building history. From the gigantic dam at Itaipu on the Amazon in South America to the flyover bridges in Alexandria in Egypt, Swiss builders are relentlessly contributing their share in enlivening the national economy.

A great economy booster for at least the past 60 years is no stranger to us. Named after its founder, Nestlé Foods Corporation has products lining most of the world's supermarket shelves. Hailed as a genius, Henri Nestlé was the first to package powdered milk and crystallised coffee. Food technology and production have taken a giant leap since then. Flavour experts concocting the latest tasty blends of fruit and vegetable extracts are deemed progressive by European standards. The quality of Swiss food remains undisputed though not unchallenged. Take, for example, the multi-talented potato, a tuber of many extraordinary tastes and textures. Available deep-frozen, it is ready for frying and roasting. Canned or vacuum-packed, it is ready to eat cold as a salad accompaniment or (microwaved) hot as an appetizing gratin. From mashed potato flakes to the chip-style baked form, Swiss food industries are hotting up their machines for more creative foods.

Commercial giants you will frequently encounter are foodstuff and non-foodstuff chains: Migros (pronounced Mi-Gro), Coop (pronounced Co-Op), Metro International, Novartis Merger (Ciba-Geigy and Sandoz merged in December 1996), Maus Frères, and Marc Rich Group, to name a few. Though not celebrated for their internationality, these companies profit well from the sheer size of their market share in Switzerland.

Banks, too, find their cult status as formidable as the number of zeros trailing after the account balance of some famous clients who bank with them. In spite of the unfortunate brouhaha over dirty cash stashed in Swiss vaults by notorious drug dealers, Swiss banks retained their savoir faire with a cool repartee – *where our clients get their money from is, frankly speaking, none of our business.* And as far as their business goes, it's still going.

When it comes to a comparison with the other nine leading industrial nations, namely Germany, France, Great Britain, Italy, Austria, United States of America, Canada, Japan and Australia, Switzerland does not shy away from competitive numbers. The smallest country out of the ten, with a population of 6.7 million permanent residents registered in 1990, Switzerland boasted a per capita output of Sfr. 32,377. Its GNP was Sfr. 312 thousand million.

The 12 largest commercial sectors' percentage share of the GNP

Trade	15.6
Building	7.7
Banks	7.1
Traffic and communications	6.7
Chemicals	4.3
Machines, equipment, vehicles	4.2
Electrical engineering	3.8
Agriculture and forestry	3.2
Hotels and catering	2.8
Metal industry	2.6
Food and luxury goods	2.5
Insurance	2.0

The Swiss economy has had its share of dips and peaks, but the recession in early 1993 did not put a damper on another bread-winning source of income – tourism. Since the time Lord George Byron (1788–1824) made his commemorative trip to Switzerland and Venice with the Shelleys, tourism has gone from strength to strength. Courtiers, viscounts, barons and baronesses, kings and queens scaled the highest mountains and tread the lowest mines. Today, visitors from all over the world trot over Swiss mountain trails, speed through motor-rail tunnels and jet about from one resort to another, contributing a satisfying 6% to the GNP (Sfr. 21,520 million of a total GNP of Sfr. 357,130 million).

RELIGION

The stuff of Zwingli and Calvin, religion is not the popular topic for discussion over three o'clock tea. Speaking about one's religion is almost as welcome as discussing one's warts and calluses. Having tried once to pry into the nature of others' belief and failing miserably, I suggest to anyone who wants to stop a conversation dead in its tracks to interject with "So what do you think about Pope John Paul II's new book [*Evangelium Vitae*] with its issues on abortion and euthanasia?" A contentious point not to be irreverently brought up by any weak-willed believer. I noticed that every time religion was mentioned, there was a discernible reluctance to explore the subject. Past association of religion with many revolutions and civil wars may be a cause for this distaste of religion as a topic of discussion.

From the rabid publicity surrounding bigots and zealots in the early 16th century, religion to many Swiss has become merely another hand-me-down tradition or culture of their forefathers. Ask a non-church-going youngster of 14 if he is Protestant, and his reply might be "yes" because his grandmother had gone to a Protestant church when she was alive.

In Zurich, where Huldrych (or Ulrich) Zwingli (1484–1531) of Wildhaus introduced reformation between 1519 and 1524, the Reformed Church of Zurich still stands as a hallmark of his humanistic teachings on puritanical simplicity. In 1522, the Zurich Council agreed on Zwingli's terms of free-preaching of the gospels forming the basis of the Church, as had the magistrates of Bern and Basel. In 1524, the Catholic cantons of Lucerne, Schywz, Uri, Unterwalden and Zug became allies against Zurich and the Reform Movement, as did the Anabaptist, or Swiss Brethren, who, under its founder Conrad Grebel (c. 1498–1526) disagreed on infant baptism and a church-state union. Evangelical-Reformists are still predominant in the Swiss-German parts of Switzerland today.

Jean Calvin (1509–1564) was a theological writer and a reformer. Born in Noyon in Picardy, France, he was exiled to Geneva and wrote the Geneva Bible, a translation of the scriptures entitled *The Quarrel, Reform, Truth, Travail and Vision.* Supplementing reformatory power with home-reformer Guillaume Farel (1489–1565), Calvin brought peace to the conflicts between the Bishops and Counts of Geneva and the reigning Dukes of Savoy.

Geneva embraced the new faith when Jean Calvin established the city as the centre of the Reformation. Influenced by Zwingli, Martin Luther and Erasmus, Calvin was hailed as the spiritual father of John Knox and credited as the originator of the dogma of Scottish Presbyterianism.

Religious civil wars and counter-reformation movements ensured constant outbreaks between Protestants and Catholics. If Heinrich Bullinger (1504–1575) was Zwingli's successor, then Theodore Beza (1519–1605) was Calvin's. In 1549, there was a union of Zwinglian and Calvinist churches, 28 years before another counter-reformation led by Carlo Borromeo was to increase internal division.

Throughout the churches' turbulent history of dissimilar thoughts and doctrines, religion in Switzerland was considered a much vilified topic. Through bloody ordeals and persecutions, religious wars spilled over to political frustration between cantons, culminating in more political chaos between liberals and Catholic conservatives.

Two latter-day Protestant theologians, Karl Barth (1886–1968) of Basel and Emil Brunner (1889–1966) of Zurich, centred some of their writings, teachings, and ethical contents on the political forefront. It is no wonder few want to get together to analyse church dogma, faced with the reality of disruptive radical reformists (or left-wing reformers).

Religion in the 20th century has taken many forms. There are Greek Orthodox and New Evangelical churches, Mormon churches, Seventh Day Adventists, Anglican chapels, Roman Catholic churches, Jewish synagogues, Buddhist temples and others. Cults have recently caused a furore in a small town called Cheiry near Geneva. Doomsday cults like the one started by Luc Jouret, a Quebecois doctor of questionable repute, had left a string of unsolved suicides in the wake of his resettling in Switzerland. After 40 people had been lured into taking their own lives and the lives of their children, many Swiss are more wary of quack religions, sending religion nosediving yet further into the denigrated doldrums.

Religious distribution

Protestant	40%
Roman Catholic	46%
Others and nondenominational	14%

POLITICS

Switzerland's political landscape is based on one of the most democratic structures known today. Because Switzerland maintains autonomous control within each of its 26 cantons, its legislative power still rests with the people. In 1848 (amended in 1874), the federal constitution converted the myriad cantons into one federal state with one common military, postal service and legislature.

The Swiss Confederation (*Schweizerische Eidgenossenschaft* or *Bund* in German) has a two-chamber legislature. They are the Federal Assembly (*Bundesversammlung* or *Assemblée Fédérale*) and the Federal Council (*Bundesrat* or *Conseil Fédéral*).

The Federal Assembly is made up of two parties: the National Council (*Nationalrat* or *Conseil National*), which represents the people, consists of 200 seats occupied by at least one representative from each canton; the Council of States (*Ständerat* or *Conseil des Etats*), which represents the cantons, consists of 46 members with two representatives from each canton making up the total.

The Federal Council is the executive power and is made up of 7 members elected by the Federal Assembly and the Federal Council to take office for a period of 4 years. The President is chosen from among the 7 (each of them from different cantons) and holds office for one year while still carrying out ministerial responsibilities. Highly respected and mostly in tune to the heartbeat of their nation, the

The Bundeshaus Parlamentsgebaude *or the Federal Parliament Building in the capital, Bern.*

presidents afore and aft have been regarded by the Swiss to be like Caesar's wife – *above* suspicion.

Decisions are made and put into Swiss law after both chambers have approved the referendums by a majority vote.

To Vote or Not to Vote – That is Not the Question

Voting is a privilege of all Swiss aged 18 and above, and they wield a fearsome influence on the political front. National policies are not carved in rock as amendments in the Swiss constitution can be contested by the People's Initiative.

Since 1891, the People's Initiative required at least 100,000 signatures for the proposal of legislation to appeal to the Federal Council. When new laws are submitted to a referendum, 30,000 disapproving Swiss is what it takes to require another vote.

A good example of putting words into action is the popular nativist movement of the 1970s. At that time, there were over a million foreigners (a petrifying 17.2% of the total population) working on fertile Swiss soil. This prompted a People's Initiative to reduce this number. As evidence that Switzerland is truly democratic, the Initiative was abruptly overturned by a National Referendum which overruled and defeated the proposal to oust alien workers.

More recently, in 1989, the People's Initiative prompted Switzerland to abolish the Swiss Army. The result: 1,052,218 voters said good riddance, but 1,903,797 said keep it. *Vox populi, vox Dei* – the voice of the people is the voice of God.

Voting for foreigners may be possible, at least for those holding a C permit and not employed as a civil servant. The Geneva government supports a change in the cantonal constitution permitting communes to grant the vote at local levels. The matter will be resolved in a referendum after 1999.

I have not personally found the Swiss too pro-liberal or excessively conservative. Their balance is a healthy one as is their view towards their government. Like myself, you may be pleasantly surprised at the lack of fuss in the way the Swiss vote on national issues – they are acutely aware of their nation's subtle changes, they are rarely misinformed, and they don't go on and on about the issue for weeks. It is as if they have understood their role in a democratic government. The question is not whether but which way to vote.

33

— Chapter Three —

THE FACTS OF LIFE

"… the tourists had gone, the rates were reduced, and there were few inducements for visitors in this small town at the water's edge, whose inhabitants, uncommunicative to begin with, were frequently rendered taciturn by the dense cloud that descended for days at a time and then vanished without warning to reveal a new landscape, full of colour and incident: boats skimming on the lake, passengers at the landing stage, an open-air market, the outline of the gaunt remains of a thirteenth century castle, seams of white on the far mountains …"

—Edith Hope, in Anita Brookner's *Hotel du Lac*

Edith Hope, writer of romantic fiction, was probably alluding to the little village at the far end of Lake Geneva; if I had to guess – Villeneuve. The 13th century castle is undoubtedly the infamous Château de Chillon, and the far mountains would be none other than the Alps. The weather is autumnal, gusty winds stripping leaves from the laurel, fig and chestnut trees along the promenades.

When people from the tropics think of vacationing in some frosty country such as Switzerland, their chief concern (and misconception) frequently has something to do with the elements. (Can you blame them if they read books like *Hotel du Lac*?) This reminds me of what my Alaskan ex-classmate used to say about dealing with their bitter cold: "If it's colder than what the Almighty had intended, He would have created sheep with synthetic fleece." Although one's comfort zone can be another's convection oven, one thing everyone looks forward to is the changing of seasons. And the best bit about the Swiss climate is the loveliness of its seasons.

CLIMATE

Not unlike most other European countries, the Swiss climate runs the whole gamut of spring, summer, autumn and winter. Generally wettish and cold with a low humidity, spring reminds me of nonexistent winters spent in a veal-coloured dormitory in 'San Franciscold'. With average temperatures rising from 10° to 15°C in Switzerland, springtime is mintily refreshing. Gardens are replanted, new buds burgeon anew and the whiteness of winter melts into a drunken daze of vermilions, yellow ochres, jade-blue purples and several hundred hues of green.

Instinctively, summer explodes onto the scene with one warm wash of sunshine. One of our favourite pastimes is to gather cherries, plums, apples and strawberries from winding routes in the hills. Joggers, cyclists, skittish rowers and swimmers rig out their accoutrements, jumpstarting the old hamstrings for a workout in the pleasant 25°C heat. The sun is always brilliant; never blistering.

Towards the tail end of summer, this hotel in Interlaken is still attracting tourists.

Autumn is my preferred season. Owing to the sweet smells of overripe fruits intoxicating the senses while visually treating one to a festive spectrum of shuddering colours, autumn is as pleasing to the senses as a crisply-baked hot apple pie on a window ledge. Temperatures fall rapidly from 25° to about 18°C, and you may have a yen for another round of barbecues, which incidentally do not stop until the fondue season comes around.

We expected our first snowfall like we expected our first child. Winter is the stuff of cheese and hot liqueurs, tobogganing and some high altitude skiing, rosy cheeks and chapped lips, indoor games and the sweet aroma of burning firewood. As the alpine Föhn sweeps up gustily from the south, the best place to be is in the company of friends, in the goodwill feeling of the Christmas season, discussing another inspiring spring.

La Tour-de-Peilz's tranquil harbour, nonchalant to adverse weather, manages to look as inviting in winter as in summer.

The last freakish winter snowed so much in La Tour-de-Peilz that making a snowman by Lake Leman was every afternoon's preoccupation. Temperatures fluctuated between –5° and about 3°C. If you lived higher, you would run into the hazard of being snowed-in for a day.

VISA AND A PERMIT TO STAY

You may be surprised no one at the customs said anything about permits. This is simply because they had not expected you to stay longer than the allowed three months as a tourist.

Check with your travel agency supplying your air ticket whether you require a visa to enter Switzerland. If you need a visa to enter, customs officers will pay more attention to your passport, your reason for coming and your departure date. Should you enter with a one-way ticket, be sure they will make a note of your address in Switzerland.

As soon as you settle down, make going to the Immigration department (which goes by different names in different cantons) a priority, but do not go empty-handed. Bring papers detailing your reasons for staying in Switzerland, either from your company or from your school. You will also need to pay a yearly administration fee of about Sfr. 70 per person. This will vary depending on which canton you settle in. You will be asked for two passport-sized photos to make the permit, which will be sent to your home about four weeks later.

With this permit, you may freely re-enter Switzerland though it only acts as proof of temporary residency. It is always a good idea to carry your passport as well at all times.

A PLACE TO CALL HOME

If you are entering Switzerland without any idea where you will eventually settle, check the local newspapers for new apartments, old apartments, chalets, converted farmhouses or houses. Staying in hotels will naturally be expensive, but don't rush into signing the contract without asking these very important questions:

1. Does the rent include central heating?
2. Assuming you will purchase a car, does it have garage facilities? How much does it cost per month?
3. Assuming you will not purchase a car, how far away are the supermarkets or local shops?
4. How long are you bound to the contract and when do you have to inform the landlord that you wish to terminate the contract?
5. Do you need a Swiss guarantor to co-sign? (This applies especially to students.)
6. Do you require a deposit? (Normally a two- to three-month rental deposit is mandatory. You will be reimbursed when the contract has ended. This will be handled by your bank and will collect interest while remaining in what is known as a *garantie-loyer*.)
7. Have you inspected the apartment thoroughly? (When you visit the apartment prior to moving in, you must do an *état des lieux*, which

is simply acknowledging the state of the place. Point out unclean areas, peeling paintwork or anything else you want the agency to note down as already damaged so that you need not be held accountable for these in the end.)

8. Have you asked who the concierge of the building is? (In case there is a faulty leak in the bathroom or the heaters won't heat up, someone else is paid to make phone calls for repairs. If there is no concierge, your agent will handle these matters. It won't hurt to ask who is the party footing the bill either.)

These pointers will invariably help you settle in better because the things you don't know will cost you most.

GETTING A PHONE

This was trickier than we had imagined. If you are moving into a brand new apartment, chances are you must have the telephone wires installed professionally. Swisscom is the place to enquire. It requires a Sfr. 1000 deposit for permit A holders but none for permit B holders. Do remember to bring your permit or your passport to show your country of birth.

On top of this deposit, you must pay a charge for installing a line. If you happen to be taking over someone else's apartment and the PTT has only officially cut off the line, all you have to do is tell them to give you the telephone number and say when you wish to have a working line and you can get both within a week. Every telephone, whether public or private, comes with IDD (International Direct Dialling) so there is only the 00 number to call in addition to the country and area code to reach the destination of your call. Every telephone directory has country code listings.

If you have not brought along your own telephone, renting one from the PTT is your best bet. Charges start from Sfr. 5.20 per month for a basic telephone; ask to see their brochure of fancy telephones or fax machines for rent or for sale. If you are sharing the telephone with someone else other than your family or merely want to know the cost of each phone call, ask them for one of those telephones with a charge counter unit. In this way, all your overseas or local calls can be budgeted fairly accurately. You could also ask for a breakdown of the length and cost of each call in your monthly phone bill, but this will cost you extra in the long run.

Alongside the cost of your telephone calls, you will be charged a monthly telephone subscription. Plainly speaking, it will cost you about Sfr. 25 per month just for the luxury of having a telephone in your home. There are services like call waiting, telephone conferencing and suppressing the ringing of an incoming call, but be warned – some of these services come with added costs.

Call 1159 to enquire the cost of calling out of Switzerland. This varies from country to country and may or may not be reduced between 10 pm and 7 am. At the end of your stay, take the receipt of your deposit and ask for the termination of your telephone line and the return of your deposit. The PTT may want this in writing, so go prepared.

ELECTRICITY

We had to put aside another Sfr. 250 to ensure we had electricity, but this could be a cantonal law in Vaud. Make sure you ask the housing agency whether there will be electricity the day you move in. Otherwise, ask them for advice on the procedure to follow.

The voltage is 220 volts, 50Hz. If, like us, your home appliances use 240 volts, you won't have to modify them for fear of having a sudden blowout.

TELEVISION AND RADIO

Mountain watching does seem rather tiresome after a month of blissful relaxation, and you will want to know what's happening in the outside world after the novelty has worn off.

Electronic appliances are pricey and dicey, but if you aren't fussy, a 14-inch television will suffice without cables and you will be able to receive three local channels: the Swiss-German SF-DRS, the Swiss-French TSR, and the Swiss-Italian RTSI. To obtain other European channels, you will need to pay the cable company. For a modest fee of Sfr. 260 per annum, we managed to hook up 22 channels.

If you happen to be a couch potato, you'll go goggle-eyed watching programmes from Germany, Italy, Austria, France, Spain, Portugal, England, and Turkey. Or while you are out shopping around for a television, you may want to own a satellite dish, impossibly commonplace to the point of being trite in Switzerland.

Skylink Switzerland can beam you English, Arabic and other European channels. You can call Skylink for yearly subscriptions through their operators. (Tel: 077/25.37.03 or 022/ 776.0391)

When you buy a brand new television set, you will likely fill out an application that alerts Billag of your purchase. Billag will then bill you about Sfr. 20 per month. You will also have to pay a fee of Sfr. 10 per month for the authorisation of private reception for your radio. Your bimonthly bill will include all these incidentals, so think again how much more you will achieve taking up a foreign language and reading the newspapers instead!

AT LA POSTE/SWISSCOM

Formerly known as the PTT, the communication services have now split. Swisscom handles all telephone/Internet services, while the Post handles mailing orders, payments via the Post Bank (if you have an account) and everything else postal. Domestic postal rates are divided into A-Post and B-Post. A-Post will be delivered by the next working day and will cost Sfr. 0.80. B-Post will cost Sfr. 0.60 and might take two to three days.

International postal rates are divided into *Prioritaire* and *Economique*. It is cheaper to send your letters or parcels to other European countries, but outside Europe, the charge for *Prioritaire* correspondence is significantly higher.

Prioritaire	*Europe*	*Outside Europe*
Under 20 g	Sfr. 1.10	Sfr. 1.80
Under 100 g	Sfr. 2.80	Sfr. 4.30
Under 200 g	Sfr. 5.00	Sfr. 7.50

Non Prioritaire	*Europe*	*Outside Europe*
Under 20 g	Sfr. 0.90	Sfr. 1.10
Under 100 g	Sfr. 1.50	Sfr. 2.00
Under 200 g	Sfr. 2.20	Sfr. 3.00

When you use the label *Par Avion*, the Post will understand it is *Prioritaire*, so make sure you have enough postage to get your mail to your destination. *Economique* is the alternative to sending heavy packages via airmail. Remember to ask about maximum dimensions and weight for the country of your destination. There are many restrictions to many countries.

The Post also offers fax services, but it can be as high as Sfr. 4 for the first A4-sized page faxed with Switzerland. Subsequent faxes cost Sfr. 0.50 each. For A4-sized pages faxed to other countries, the first page costs Sfr. 9 and each subsequent page costs Sfr. 5.

If a registered letter or parcel arrives for you, the Post in your commune will drop an orange slip into your mailbox requesting your presence with your passport or permit for collection. You are invited to collect your parcel or letter within 7 days; bring the slip with you for verification.

Guidelines are printed every 1 January listing the tariffs for different destinations, durations and any other limitations for sizes, weights and taxes as well as international commercial responses and registered mail. EMS is an international courier service you can employ to send your correspondence *tout de suite* in Europe (it takes 24–48 hours) or elsewhere in the world (24–72 hours).

The Post is a bank and also the place to pay your bills with a green chit called *versement*, normally placed beside the cashier's window. You can pay your gas bills using a *versement*. Yellow booklets used to be issued for stamping payments, but this is not doen anymore.

THE SWISSCOM

If you need a new line for Internet access, then Swisscom is the place to enquire. If you need a cellphone (or *natel,* as the Swiss call them), drop by one of the many Swisscom outlets and pick a snazzy little number. You can call 0800 800 113 (toll-free) if you want to enquire about their communications services or costs, but unless you're fluent in the language of the region, it's far more productive to actually visit the shop and make your enquiries personally. Taxcards that go into the Swisscom phones have rendered coinphones obsolete. You can purchase these cards in denominations of Sfr. 2, 10 or 20 from almost any Tabac, train station, restaurant (ask the waiter/waitresses) or hotel.

INSURANCE

I shudder to contemplate life in Switzerland without insurance. Insurance is the lesser of two evils – you either pay through your nose or pay your insurance company.

As you settle into your apartment, you will receive a letter from the canton requesting you to detail the cost of your furniture, your electronic equipment and everything else, right down to the cost of your entire wardrobe, for insurance purposes. This means you will be covered in case a freak fire breaks out or some unforeseen natural disaster wreaks havoc in your home. The cost of this type of home insurance is minimal coverage. We had to pay a yearly amount of Sfr. 10 to cover everything we owned. If you desire to cover theft or loss of your equipment, or in case your 5-year-old throws a rock through your neighbour's window, you should ask what different insurance coverage can be made available to you.

Health or accident insurance is also mandatory. The average Swiss devotes about 10% of his household expenditure to doctors, dentists, health insurance and medicine. What this proposes to do is take the burden of payment from the individual to the insurance company. For example, doctors' consultation fees run from Sfr. 50 upwards, but you will be reimbursed by your insurance company if you are covered. I would strongly advise you to purchase your accident insurance in your home country if it's possible. However, health insurance can run up a long bill if you are treated in an outpatient facility. Unless you are prone to illnesses, you need not purchase an expensive health insurance policy.

Car insurance will be discussed two sections down for those bent on getting a car.

BUT FIRST, HOW TO GET SOME WHEELS

Almost everyone owns wheels – if not on a car, then a moped (motorised bicycle), if not a moped, a bicycle, and if not a bicycle, at least a cool pair of rollerblades, or rollerskates. Buying any of these things should not be your idiomatic leap in the dark because you have many opportunities to pick and choose what you like.

The newspapers are an endless source of advertisements to buy or sell. Cars of every shape, size, power and brand can be found in many of the local or national tabloids. Cars are left-hand drive and are driven on the right of the road, much like the rest of Europe with the exception of the United Kingdom and Ireland. If you are not yet fluent with the language of your locality, find someone who can help you bargain.

Perhaps one of the disadvantages in getting a car from someone other than from the dealer is the distinct inconvenience of not getting the papers done for you. Any vehicle with four wheels will require you to obtain the right papers before you are even allowed to drive it. You will therefore need to ask the seller of the vehicle all these questions:

1. How much does the car registration cost?
2. Can you help me change my international driver's licence into a Swiss driver's licence? (If you are staying in Switzerland for more than a year.)
3. How much is the road tax for this vehicle?
4. Has the car gone through an 'expertise'? An 'expertise' means the car has passed a thorough examination and been given a clean bill of health. I advise you to purchase a car that has been recently 'expertised'.
5. How do I get a *permis de circulation*? This is a grey leaflet that gives you authorisation to drive the car. Make sure you have this with your insurance papers before you take off into the sunset. The *permis de circulation* will be the first thing police who stop you on the road ask for.
6. Can you recommend a car insurance company?

Buying a moped or bicycle is simpler, but both will also require registration and some form of insurance coverage.

If you need to go on the highway, don't forget to purchase your *autoroute vignette* at the PTT, service station or frontier post. It costs Sfr. 40 and always lasts 14 months until 31 January of the next year.

And don't forget to buckle up – this applies to both front and back passengers in a car. Children under 12 are not allowed in the front passenger seat.

Speed limits:
50 km/h in built-up areas
80 km/h on roads outside built-up areas
120 km/h on motorways

Insuring Your Vehicle

Insuring your vehicle is costly. I shall not mince words but come straight to where it will hurt most – your pocketbook. Small cars are rampant in Switzerland, especially in cities or university towns. Larger family sedans like the Volvos or the Mercedes are quite the norm as well. Naturally it stands to reason that the more powerful your vehicle, the costlier your insurance.

There are two main types of insurance: The first is called the RC (F: *Responsabilité civile* / G: *Haftpflichtversicherung* / I: *Assicurazione Responsabilita Civile*); if you have this, your insurance company will cover the cost of damages that you have inflicted upon another vehicle. Ask to see if they pay only a percentage after exceeding a certain limit.

The second choice you have is a *Casco complet*, or full comprehensive insurance. This will cover damages inflicted on you by hit-and-runners, hooligans, vandals, or nature itself. It naturally costs the most. It is a good idea to ask your friends or colleagues which insurance company they know is worthy of earning your annual premium of Sfr. 2000–3000 for this kind of insurance.

There is also the partial comprehensive which insures against all risks except that of collisions. This is good if your car is a jalopy and not worth the full comprehensive. If you are not sure how much your car is worth, you can call the Touring Club of Switzerland (022/786.09.92) for a routine check-up. Founded in 1896, TCS provides free towing services, where a mechanic will jumpstart your car and

Electrically run, anti-polluting buses bring passengers from Villeneuve to Vevey. Here the bus stops in Montreux, home to the Rose d'Or International television competition. (Photo by Charles Eu)

perform a myriad of other car-related services. TCS membership costs Sfr. 40 per year plus a Sfr. 10 admission fee. A second card for your spouse costs an additional Sfr. 20. TCS membership entitles you primarily to servicing your vehicle if there is a breakdown, tow-away assistance and covering the cost of getting you home.

What about Buses and Underground Trains?

The buses in Switzerland are very efficient and clean. They are punctual and singlehandedly operated by the driver, and some are electrically run. You pay before getting on if there is a ticketing machine at the bus stop, otherwise you can purchase your ticket either from the driver or from the automated machine at the back of the bus. There is an additional cost for bringing dogs on buses.

Underground travel (called the métro) is lightweight transport confined to larger cities like Zurich, Geneva, Basel, Lausanne, etc. Prices of tickets depend on the length of the journey and zones travelled; they are lower for senior citizens, students and those with discounted fare cards.

SAFETY IN SWITZERLAND

The first time my father called to see if we had landed safely in Switzerland, I noted the unusual calm that accompanied his voice over the crackly receiver. The previous years spent in the dog-eat-dog world of Los Angeles had gripped me with a kind of fascinating fear. Now I answered with cogent delight that Switzerland was as safe as a goldfish in a goldfish bowl. Little did I realise then the truth of that left-handed compliment.

After our first year in Glion-sur-Montreux, where the only cause for distress were the early bleats and bell-ringings from the mountain goats, we discovered a new phenomenon just emerging from the tip of the financial iceberg – recession.

You don't have to be a highly trained sociologist to determine that many of the world's social problems are a direct domino result of the steady loss of jobs and low self-esteem brought about by recession. Vandalism, hooliganism and alcoholism have been on the rise, as well as drug abuse and teen suicides. Though not currently the highest in Europe, Switzerland has its share of problems dealing with the rise in unemployment. Heed the following advice, which I will give my children, and my children's children – don't go looking for trouble by jogging in the dead of night, or court disaster by swimming alone in some lake. And above all, know what's going on around you. You will only be as safe as you are uninformed in a seemingly harmless fishbowl.

OPENING AND CLOSING HOURS

Banks open early and close early, from 8:30 am to 4:30 pm Monday through Friday. As a rule, all shops and boutiques close during lunchtime, which is around 12:30 to 1:30 pm. Only restaurants and larger department stores remain open during the lunch hour.

Switzerland divides its working hours between the summer-autumn months and the winter-spring months. On weekdays in the hotter months, you will find stores open from 9 am until 6:30 pm. Greengrocers, confectioners, bakers, butchers and other small businesses open as early as 7:30 am. The Post also open their automatic doors at 9 am, closing them at 6:30 pm sharp. Smaller post offices close during lunchtime, so take note of the hours, usually at the entrance of the building. Saturdays are partial working days, so supermarkets and boutiques all close at 5 pm.

In the colder months at the end of winter and in early spring, stores and shops generally close earlier, but this is subject to change depending on the number of tourists or the weather. As a general rule, Thursday nights are late shopping nights, and shops close at 8 pm.

Libraries, museums and cinemas have different opening and closing hours which vary with the seasons. Museums are normally closed on Mondays and cinemas do not open until late afternoon or evening. Restaurants cater to their guests from 11:30 am until 2 pm for lunch and usually from 6:30 pm until 9 pm for dinner. Bistros often serve light snacks such as sandwiches, pastries and teacakes throughout the day.

Unorthodox eateries, including kebab stalls, sidewalk sandwicheries and confectionaries (or *Konditoreien*) are frequented by locals as well as foreigners. These offer a variety of light meals. An enjoyable teatime practice of mine is to sit in a cafeteria of a large shopping mall, nibbling on an apple turnover and sipping a scalding hot cup of coffee over my favourite newspapers.

PUBLIC HOLIDAYS

1 January	New Year's Day
April	Good Friday
April	Lundi de Pâques (Easter Monday)

1 May	Labour Day (in certain cantons)
May	Corpus Christi (in Roman Catholic cantons)
June	Ascension Day falls on the Thursday, 40 days after Easter, while Pentecostal Monday falls 50 days after Easter
18 June	Fête-Dieu (in certain cantons)
1 August	Swiss National Day
15 August	Assumption Day (in certain cantons)
1 November	Toussaint (in certain cantons)
6 December	St. Nicholas' Day (in certain cantons)
8 December	The Immaculate Conception (in Roman Catholic cantons)
25 December	Christmas Day

Note: In Switzerland, when a holiday falls on a Sunday, the Monday that follows is a holiday.

SHOPPING

The house is immaculate, you've purchased your dinky three-door Renault, the phone has been hooked up and there is electricity. Now to stock up your *frigo* with some goodies.

Almost any smart-shopping *madame* or *Frau* will direct you to the nearest neighbourhood Migros, part of the largest supermarket chain in Switzerland. Founded by Gottlieb Duttweiler (1888–1962), Migros really began as stores-on-wheels bringing staples from the producer to the buyers at street corners. Later, regular stores were opened and these grew into the chain that was to link up rapidly with other communities to make Migros a household word.

The size of a Migros supermarket is determined by the number of M's printed outside the shop. The largest Migros, usually found in densely populated residential areas or just immediately outside the city, will advertise 'Migros MMM'. The smallest Migros in the sticks will have only one 'M'. At a Migros MMM, you will find the entire range of household products, foods, titbits, stationery, clothing, pet foods, some hardware tools and electrical appliances. Gardening tools, plants and even an ample variety of do-it-yourself materials can be found. This is also the place to drop off your negatives for developing. Photo developing can be expensive in photo supply shops (usually Sfr. 1 per standard-sized glossy, not including developing), so either send them to the laboratory or let the clerk send them for you.

Another familiar supermarket chain is Coop, which is slightly more expensive than Migros. Coop supermarkets stock foreign food-stuffs such as tacos and salsas, Chinese sauces, exotic condiments and Indian spices not found on Migros shelves. Most people do not discriminate between the two largely because it is nice to have an alternative other than Migros to go to. I go to Coop for the speciality foodstuff after buying the usual fare at Migros.

Each Migros or Coop outlet has different pricing from sister branches owing to location. For example, if the Migros in the sleepy Fribourg outskirts charges Sfr. 0.60 for a red pepper, the one in touristy downtown Interlaken may sell the same produce for Sfr. 0.70.

Other supermarkets you will encounter are Denners, Pick and Pay (they have a good variety of liquor), Innovation, Waro, and Placette. Speciality shops like Globus stock gourmet products, including oddly-twisted pretzels from South America and original couscous from Algeria. Better are your chances of finding imported Japanese seaweed appetisers or English tea biscuits if you've got a craving you can't squish.

Window-shopping is a favourite pastime of people here, as elsewhere: traipsing down aisles requires little effort. Here is a list of places to browse in on days your grey cells go on strike. The pricing is listed as very expensive, expensive, moderate, average or inexpensive.

ABM – Stationery, haircare products, fabrics, household, fingerfoods (average to inexpensive)

Ausoni – By the Ausoni brothers, tailored suits, French and Italian labels (expensive)

Bally – The ultimate Swiss shoestore (expensive to moderate)

Benetton – The famous Italian preppy rainbow-coloured fashion store (expensive)

Bon Genie – Top-end boutique brands such as Lacroix, Gigli, Hugo Boss, etc. (very expensive)

C & A – Good bargains for men and women's apparel (average)

City-disc – Your basic music store for CDs, cassettes, videos, vinyls, and audio equipment (average)

Conforama – Furniture store for those who cannot afford Ikea (average)

EPA – Clothing, household, foodstuff, some electrical appliances, toys (average to inexpensive)

Esprit – An American import, the clothes are comfortable but the prices can be most uncomfortable (expensive)

Globus – The same name as the speciality food store, this Globus sells men's wear from executive cuts and polo T-shirts to leather jackets and adventure wear (moderate to expensive)

Hennes & Mauritz – The shop most young female adults frequent for their ultra miniskirts and lacy lingerie, H & M, as its outlets are affectionately known, is the best mid-price clothing store with the most up-to-date fashions (average to moderate)

Ikea – Furniture store from Sweden that covers the A to Z in home furnishing, another excellent place to shop for wedding presents (moderate)

Innovation – Clothing, perfumes, stationery, handbags, televisions, radios, glassware, kitchen utensils, crockery and children's toys (moderate)

Intersound – Visual and audio equipment store plus electronic games (average to inexpensive)

Jelmoli – Clothing and shoestore (average)

Kitch'n'Cook – As the name suggests, this store in Bern specialises in kitchenware such as crockery, cutlery and aprons. An excellent place to buy a wedding gift (moderate to very expensive)

Kramers – Stationery, photo developing, art materials, oils, acrylics, pastels, typewriters, cards (above average prices)

Merkur – Confectionery with a wide range of chocolates, sweets, truffles and gift ideas. Larger Merkur outlets also have a *Konditorei*, or a small cafe where you can sample some *petits fours* (moderate)

Payot – Books and magazines (average)

Placette – The most comprehensive departmental store (moderate)

Swatch shop – For those indispensable fashion statements for your wrist, Swatch (or Swiss watch) is worn by young and old, rich and poor (standardised prices: moderate to average)

Swisscom – Telecommunications shop galore. For pagers, cellular phones (Natel), Garfield-shaped phones and applications for phone lines.

Volger – Women's clothes and shoeshop (inexpensive to average)

SWISS CURRENCY

In orange, blue and green, Swiss Franc (or CHF) notes come in 10's, 20's, 50's, 100's, 500's and 1000's. Each franc is divided into 100 centimes or rappen. Small change will come in a jangle of 5's, 10's, 20's, 50's, 1 Frs, 2 Frs and 5 Frs. Strangely enough, many Swiss still prefer to pay cash through the Post even though a giro transfer system exists. In supermarkets, a bank card is occasionally used, but you will not find a chequebook in sight.

RECYCLING

The Swiss are radical recyclists. From recycling aluminium cans to glass and PET bottles, old newspapers, annuals, directories, furniture, batteries, clothing and nature itself (composting), it appears that the

Recycling is not for eco-faddists; it is a way of life. Different coloured glassware is separated in large bins before collection.

thrifty Swiss are far ahead of the other European countries, with the exception of Germany.

A clever idea locals have for recycling furniture is to put out their old broken chairs and beds and whatnots onto the street one day in the month. People of all classes seem to take a shining to collecting these discarded goodies come chilly winter or breezy autumn. Winter tyres, children's bicycles, wardrobes and flower pots are scrutinised by avid handymen who will literally load up their trucks with these less-than-perfect recyclables. Personally, scrounging around for bar stools or a CD rack is a rather humbling experience, but pouring through the mountain of knickknacks, it has often surprised the husband and me to find rather splendid stuff – some in fact you might find at the flea markets with a price tag on them. When you are in Switzerland, it pays to recycle.

Chapter Four

FOLKLORE GALORE AND ENTERTAINMENT TODAY

The writer-philosopher Rousseau once said, *"Tout n'est pas abominable, infernal, sauvage dans les Alpes. C'est vivable, habité, cultivé,"* which to us Anglophones simply means "All is not abominable, infernal, or savage in the Alps. It is livable, habitated and cultivated." Switzerland has one of the richest folklores in Europe and, ethnographically speaking, can fill the entire Musée de l'Homme in Paris.

There are nearly 20 traditional carnivals parading about their narrow streets every year, from the superbly decked-out Carnival de Bâle (or the Basler-Morgestraich) to the Lundi Gras (as opposed to Mardi Gras, which means Shrove Tuesday, or literally 'Fat Tuesday') in Lucerne. Mighty paganistic, painted masks and colourful costumes, tubas, tambourines, fifes and empty cans promise to make a cacophony that will be savage to your ears. The origin of some carnivals is rooted in pre-Christian times: such is the Appenzell Sylvesterklause or the Roitschäggätä in the Lötschental, where fierce hobgoblin-like masks are worn.

There is also an unspoken pride of the artisans, which many Swiss identify with: an object well crafted, time well spent, work well done; by men who spend nearly 40 years of their lives as furniture craftsmen, metal workers, keymakers, or butter moulders. Wooden sculptures of bears, pressed edelweiss, mountain bells, cowbells the size of a cow's head, barrel bells, wind chimes, cuckoo clocks, mountain landscapes painted on linen, embroidery, suspenders and beer mugs all reek of some artist's studio. It's what people come to Switzerland for, apart from stuffing their backpacks with Swatches and Swiss army knives.

Monumentalism is not a rare trait of the artisans; in fact, it is a common sight. Large armour, swords, sleighs, or the monstrous applepress at Stein am Rhein seem to have been made for gargantuan gaillards. Metal workers made extraordinarily complicated oversized clocks. Yet it is not entirely true to say that the Swiss live in the past because they preserve their traditions well. They don't always troop up to Val D'Herens for the exciting cow fights instead of spending a quiet evening in the theatre. Nor do they excessively pursue *schwingen* (alpine wrestling), yodelling, country folk band-playing or grape harvesting. Entertainment today has only broadened to include much of what the country is already blessed with. In summer, every open hillside is a stage – jazz festivals alternate with alphorn and string folk bands, film stars and rock bands rub shoulders with Italian tenor

Pavarotti and French mood music maestro Jean-Jacques Jarre. From folklore galore to entertainment today, we found a lot more than television hacking or playing on the Super Nintendo Mario Brothers.

NEWSPAPERS AND JOURNALS

One of the most fiendish delights university undergraduates have is to frequent the newspaper kiosks, where you can easily mistake their newspapers and magazines for the wallpaper decoration. Such kiosks are as inexhaustible a conservatory of pop information as the library is of educational resources.

Switzerland has over 400 daily and weekly newspapers with a total circulation in excess of 3.5 million. You may not find all 400 in one kiosk, but those available promise to pique your mental faculties to the maximum. Switzerland's first newspaper, the *Wochenzeitung*, appeared in Basel in 1610. The local tabloid *Blick* leads the Swiss pack in its quest for more news while *24 Heures*, *La Suisse*, *Basler Zeitung*, *Die Wochen Zeitung* and *Tages Anzeiger* seem content to roll off the presses into the dentist's waiting room. The average cost of dailies is about Sfr. 2 and most of them contain mostly the happenings of countries in Europe.

English language newspapers are found at almost any newsagent. The British *Guardian* sells for Sfr. 3.60, while *USA Today* goes for about Sfr. 3.50. Other broadsheets include *The Independent*, *The International Herald Tribune*, *The European* and *The Financial Times*. *Swiss News*, a locally published business-cum-cultural magazine, costs Sfr. 8.50 – expensive if you are buying it for the cultural bits.

Far from being cruelly limited to certain types of magazines and newspapers, most newsagents insist on carrying the bulk of gossip tabloids, crossword puzzles, and naughty, flirty pornos. Europeans are perhaps so inundated with the copiousness of printed glossies that young teens can be seen openly discussing certain well-endowed private parts. Fashion, architecture, home improvement, sports, cars, trains, boats, food, executive lifestyles, astrology, religion, the Queen of England and the House of Windsor, celebrities, computers – multiply these by four languages and you'll have a dizzy variety of choice at the kiosk.

ART AND CULTURE

The hallmark of one's traditions, Swiss art and culture is an interesting amalgamation of folklore and handicraft. Expressed in woodcuts, embroidery, ceramics, basketry, stained-glass windows, old inn signs, copperware and peasant art, each regales a history of long sufferance and perseverance. There are numerous museums exhibiting contemporary folk art. The Arts Council of Switzerland in Zurich publishes a range of books that may prove a rich source of information if you are the type who likes to forage about for something a little recherché. (Write or call Pro Helvetia, Hirschengraben 22, CH-8024 Zurich. Tel: 01-251-9600.)

Among the other 540-over museums scattered throughout the country, the most popular and indeed only National Museum in Zurich, called the Schweizerisches Landesmuseum, is an excellent place to visit. To understand life in Switzerland in depth and totality, I should advise you to take a weekend trip there. This is one museum important enough not to miss.

Many fans of Jean Tinguely would be pleased to find his works in outdoor parks and open spaces. Born in Fribourg in 1925, Tinguely is a sculptor of plastic iron art – fantastic motorised machines made from scrap metal. Tinguely never lost his creative prowess in graphic design even well into the late 1970s. When he married Niki St. Phalle, a celebrated artist and sculptor in her own right, Switzerland suddenly found a handsome pair of artists who made contemporary art an avant garde thing. Bernhard Luginbühl is another name you will encounter in Swiss sculpture.

With all due respect to those truly interested in the arts and cultural movements in Switzerland, the Swiss did not seriously ride on the mammoth waves of influence till much later, to the chagrin of many

On the top floor of MAMCO are the temporary exhibits. Tony Smith's sculptures lure art aficionados into the world of Abstractism.

of the local artists. Undaunted by the lack of response, the inimitable Paul Klee, born in Münchenbuchsee near Bern, Max Bill, Ferdinand Hodler, Felix Vallotton and Alberto Giacometti had to make their mark elsewhere. During the time when the Universités des Beaux-Arts and salons were clamouring for more Picassos and Matisses, many Swiss were drawn by the sheer energy and vibrancy of such an art mecca. From the turn of the century onwards, many still make their pilgrimage to Paris's Louvre, Pompidou and Musée d'Orsay to see something that Swiss artists such as Paul Klee had created during the turbulent 1920s.

Visiting MAMCO (Musée d'art Moderne et Contemporain) in Geneva with my husband's class in Contemporary Art History, I discovered much to my surprise the extensive modern collection of installation art from Joseph Kosuth to Barbara Kruger. There were the myriad and the varied, conscientiously well amassed works of art from Europe hanging on the wall or glued to the floor. The Kunsthaus in Basel is another such museum; make this your second weekend trip into the art world for a memorable lesson in modern and fine art.

On the whole, museums in Switzerland are made more conspicuous by their absence of publicity. Those who venture into the corridors of the art world are virtually all tourists, or expatriates interested in finding something else to do on a weekend. Don't lose heart though, because in spite of the rarity of museums in some places, Switzerland can usually spare a chalet to house something terribly interesting and such places are quite exact as to the nature of their exhibits. For example, the Museum of Photography focuses on photography. Likewise, the Musée d'alimentation in Vevey (owned by Nestlé) specifically exhibits the history of food or anything connected with the food industry and its manufacturing process. The Museum of Horology in La Chaux-de-Fonds explains every aspect of watchmaking and time-ticking in minute detail. The Basel Paper Mill and the Toy Museum, Village and Viniculture Museum of Riehen are exquisite gems of museums little considered compared to the Kunstmuseum or Kunsthalle. I hasten to add, however, that many of the explanations pinned to the exhibits are not in English. Do remember to pick up your copy (not always free) detailing the various types of artwork in the language of your preference.

There are many more museums not listed here. Locating interesting museums in Switzerland is rather like looking for truffles, but you don't need a pig. All you need is a good nose for sniffing out obscure museums in a tiny tucked-away corner in a village.

Literature

Browsing through the stiffened spines of hardcovers in the *bibliothèque municipale de Vevey* one Tuesday afternoon, I chanced upon an extremely used copy of *Corinne* by Madam de Staël. There were at least five shelves of Swiss authors sitting pertinently there for all to admire. Alas, the most dog-eared books are not authored by the Swiss.

Books by French authors, I was told, were those regularly checked out, at least in the Swiss-Romande parts.

Swiss-Romande authors have been waging a perilous war with their neighbouring French writers, who of course deem their French the authorised and more grammatically correct version than Swiss French. Those who escape being harangued must include Charles-Ferdinand Ramuz (1878–1947), who wrote *La Grand Peur dans la montagne* (Terror in the mountains), and Blaise Cendrars (1887–1961), who penned *Les Pâques à New York* (Easter in New York).

Many of Ramuz's beloved characters are set in French-speaking Switzerland. He spins homely yarns about the average middle income people, with staunch and modest heroes and heroines full of backbone and guts. Fighting loneliness seems to be a recurring theme in many of his novels, and if it were not for his skill in portraying realism in his characters, many might have deemed his writing too melancholy.

Born nine years after Ramuz is Blaise Cendrars, who couldn't have been more different from Ramuz in sentiments about Switzerland. An adventurous and free-spirited writer and poet, Cendrars left behind a legacy of thought-provoking poetry replete with startling images and novels that reflected the restrictive nature of Switzerland.

These authors, like those Swiss artists long unrecognised in their country as well as on the continent, are practising geniuses who were far ahead of their time.

Other notable authors whose works are not usually found upon dustless shelves are Jean-Jacques Rousseau, Gottfried Keller, Conrad-Ferdinand Meyer, Friedrich Dürrenmatt and popular playwright Max Rudolf Frisch. Representing a new generation of writers who make local bookworming a reincarnated hobby are Jacques Chappaz and Hugo Loetscher.

Dialect literature or literature written in the oral tradition is a speciality that few can say they have tried, or even *want* to try. Swiss Italian authors such as Alina Borioli and Giovanni Bianconi, and Swiss German authors including Kurt Marti and Mani Matter are some of the few who wrote in their own dialects. Both Marti and Matter has written in Berndeutsche but Kurt Marti also has works in German. Many of these works are insightful and deeply personal, and reflect their yearning for an identity within themselves. Difficulty in making their mark as writers ultimately urged these Swiss writers to seek recognition on foreign soil.

Franziska, a dear friend of ours, is typical of a trend that has become a Swiss way of life – she reads voraciously 400-page novels of all translated sorts by the lake in summer. If I had to guess, I would say that the Swiss are not one-minded in their appetites for different cultures. They have got three to contend with in the first place. My heart goes out to those struggling to publish their writing. Just strive on: if you cannot make it anywhere else, you'll make it in Switzerland.

Music and Theatre

The first time I heard the name Ernest Ansermet was during French lessons on the topic of outstanding Swiss conductors. He was the resident conductor of the *Orchestre de la Suisse Romande* and the blue-eyed boy of the classical music scene.

Having founded the orchestra in 1918, it was primarily due to Ansermet that French music filled the auditoriums of theatres instead of the then much accepted Viennese atonal and serial works. As one walks by Lake Leman near the mouth of a torrential river, *quai Ansermet* is the one place full of music in the summertime as families gather together for a picnic and a stroll in the park.

Swiss music had had the benefit of foreign patronage, especially from the Germans and French. Most composers teach music in order to survive as did famous music maestros Pierre Boulez and Vladimir Vogel. The large number of conservatories is a direct result of the pedagogical nature of music lovers of that era. The conservatory in Geneva will have to pay Franz Liszt credit, for shortly after his term there, conservatories sprouted up in Basel, Fribourg, Bienne,

Winterthur, Zurich, Lucerne and Lausanne.

Arthur Honegger (1892–1955) founded the Swiss Association in 1900 and achieved fame through his *Roi David* oratorium in 1912. To this day, Honegger remains a beloved character, remembered as a *compositeur terrifiant* by those in the music world. There is a distinct intensity in the diverse cultural and theatrical aspects in Switzerland. Twentieth century Swiss composer Othmar Schoeck (1886–1957) merged romantic poetry with opera, producing *Penthesilea* and *Das Schloss Durande* as two of his most memorable stage works.

Younger composers from the pop art culture of the sixties, including Rudolf Kelterborn, Heinz Holliger and Michel Tabachnik, now play a tune of their own, leaving invisible traces of their Swiss identities. Where once Swiss music was a synthesis of French and German musical cultures, the latter-day compositions stand independent of them and are unique creations.

Having been absolutely barraged by tons of glossy brochures on unique Swiss folklore festivals, one which bears mention must be the open-air production of Friedrich Schiller's *William Tell* in the Rugen Woods near Interlaken. Old traditions die hard and this legendary myth of the 13th century marksman and his young assistant son is no exception. Kept alive possibly by tourists who find the tale exceptionally endearing, thousands flock to this pretty summer resort in July to watch the play re-enacted by 200-odd actors plus animal extras.

Another extraordinary festival bound to send you writing home is the Swiss Folk Costume and Alpine Herdsmen's Festivals. You can't get much more rustic than this. Among the events held in Interlaken in August are Alpine wrestlers *schwingen* (Alpine wrestling) and brawny men throwing 83.5 kg stones – far more exciting than watching Arnold Schwarzenneger flex his biceps on a blue screen.

The Festspiel marks the celebration of a festival or event with costumed locals dancing and making merry music. Another delight to tourists and to their own native kinsfolk is the *männerchor*, which can consist of four male voices – called a quartet – to a chorus of plenty.

Watching it on television provides hardly any atmosphere for what can be a joyous celebration.

The recent addition of the Bejart Ballet in Lausanne in 1987 is worthy of mention. Founded by Frenchman Maurice Bejart, then with his own company in the Belgian capital of Brussels, he has since that time been hailed as a Mephistophelian ballet choreographer extraordinaire. Considering Swiss ballet has only carved a niche for itself in the last 30 years, Bejart's ground-breaking *Souvenirs de Leningrad* was followed by the equally emotive *Rite of Spring* in 1992.

Japan has the *kabuki*, India the *Bhakti*, but Switzerland has enough growing talent to make certain that ballet soirées remain a lasting influence on the musical, theatrical, and operatic forefront.

Movies

Returning to the USA in 1999, I figured watching the *Rugrats* movie with my three-year old was tantamount to sacrificing a fine lunch at the Olive Tree Restaurant. The prospect of that sounded way too foolish even for a doting mum. Returning to Switzerland and discovering that the price of a ticket had upped Sfr. 4 since 1995 was not entirely shocking. It simply meant I'd never see the inside of a cinema ever again.

But it's impossibly hard to restrain oneself when everyone else goes and suffers the consequences of dry toast and water for the next few days. V.O. (original version) movies are popular with the Swiss and a sociable way to unwind. Movies are uncensored but have a rating system that only parents are interested in. The average cost of watching a movie is about Sfr. 12 for students and Sfr. 15 for adults.

Many aficionados of the big screen opt to buy a carnet of tickets (10 in all, valid for 12 months) for a cheaper price. Some cinemas under the Metrociné name offer a discount card, but of course this only works if you watch the movie at their outlets. To all diehard celluloidian fans, I leave you this advice – think video and a good surround-sound stereo in your television.

Jazz Festivals

When I read what the English poetess Anne Howard said of culture improving fruits of the human mind, it made me think immediately of the 1994 jazz festival held in Montreux. Since the beginning of the jazz era, this particular jazz festival, an American import of the 1920s, has broadened musical talents and educated people on world music beyond jazz as we all know it. Not only does the Montreux festival make toe-tapping, shoulder-shaking, finger-snapping a permanent twitch during the two to three weeks in July, it has evolved into hip-flinging, body-worming and arm-flapping aerobic exercise in the Auditorium Stravinsky and Miles Davis Hall.

A cool summery breeze brought just the right temperature to stroll along Lake Leman with the husband and our best friend Dominique.

Cars spelling out their licences from as far away as Aargau and Ticino were already lining up the *rue du lac* from Clarens to Territet. A scroll of choice bands from virtual unknowns to pop evergreens lured anyone who had heard of this sacred event to shell out something like eighty francs for a night at the auditorium. Those who just wanted to feel involved without feeling the pinch sat by the lake and listened to hip bands doing the Megadeath impression of leaving ringing in your ears. International mega-celebrities like Quincy Jones, Herbie Hancock, Bobby McFerrin, Natalie Cole, Van Morrison, Dwight Yoakam, and Simply Red were the names on everybody's lips. Tickets were sold at the booths outside the auditorium, at the Swiss Bank Corporation (the one with the three keys) or among scores of ticketing outlets throughout Switzerland.

Similar jazz festivals in Nyon, Bern, Zurich, Lucerne or Lugano are not unheard of. The organisers are adept at importing a healthy mixture of jazz, blues, country, pop, rock, fusion, world, electronic (Yanni and Jarre), a capella, folk and even gospel.

The popularity of jazz festivals grows each summer, so keep your eyes peeled for their advertisements. Any music outlet like a CD or video store is bound to plaster their front doors with the fortnight's events.

After forking out eighty francs each, we finally exited close to two in the morning. The night was definitely still young. Throngs of young ones were sardined in the pubs. Those who were not performing that night were jamming something serious on the electric guitar and synthesizer. It was infectious, this thronging in the pub with your friends. The Swiss are hardly snobbish with their choice of music, for they are not weary of the obnoxious display of chamber music nor are they sickened to the headbanging Beavis-and-Butthead cacophony on MTV.

Don't be surprised to find the crowd at Bejart's ballet the same rowdy bleary-eyed bunch in the pub the night before.

Music Festivals worth parting with your money for:
Ascona: Music Festival Weeks (Sep-Oct)
Bern: International Jazz Festival (mid-Jun)
Braunwald Music Weeks (Jul-Aug)
Engadine Concert Weeks (Jul-Aug)
Gstaad: Yehudi Menuhin Festival (Aug)
Lausanne Italian Opera Festival (Oct)
Lugano: Estival Jazz and the New Orleans Jazz Festival (Jun-Jul)
Lucerne: International Festival of Music (Aug-Sep)
Montreux: International Choral Festival (Apr); Montreux-Vevey
Nyon: Paleo Festival (mid-Jul)
International Music Festival (Sep)
Sion: Tibor Varga Music Festival (Jul-Sep)
Zurich: International Jazz Festival (Oct)

Radio stations worth listening to:
WRG-FM World Radio Geneva 88.4 MHz
Radio 74 International Station 88.8 MHz

— Chapter Five —

SKI, SURF, SUN AND SKINCARE

The Swiss are blessed with a country where the terrain provides ample opportunity for sports to be part and parcel of The Good Life. The reason why their postcards and calendars look so appealing is because the real thing is twice as dreamy. These commercial goodies have not been doctored or glossed over, I can assure the most suspicious foreigner.

The first time we took the *funiculaire*, a cog-wheeled electric carriage that moves steeply up the mountain, we found ourselves 700 metres up in Glion agog at the supremacy of the view. Man can level a mountain, but to create one requires the omnipotence of the Divine.

Switzerland is the playground of adventurous Europeans avid for more treacherous sports. The climate is suited seasonally to a variety of activities and to be bored by the countless sporting events can only mean one is deadly dull beyond redemption.

WHAT TO DO IN WINTER
(mid December to end March)

Mountain skiing is something you can do all year round, even in summer when most of the snow has melted at 2,400 metres. Arriving in a skicamp in Switzerland, one must be prepared to take its sports to heart. Half-baked sportsmen normally end up chowing down cheese fondue at the local inns. With more than 200 ski resorts, you don't just go blindly to the information bureau and ask for directions to the nearest indoor tennis courts.

Skiing is every bit as Swiss as cricket was to British colonials in India. Although mountain skiing is the obvious choice for winter decathloners and thrill-seekers alike, it would be foolhardy to trail-

Ask for the 'baby' downhill slope if you are a beginner.

69

blaze your winter away without attempting cross-country skiing, tobogganing, skikjöring or simply hiking.

Cross-country Skiing (G: Langlauf / F: Ski de fond)

Unlike mountain skiing, where you careen your way down the blue (elementary), red (intermediate) or black slopes (amateurs, remove yourselves), cross-country skiing is more an aerobic workout with a view to boot. The skis are usually narrower and the shoes more comfortable. There could be more than one ski circuit depending on the size of the resort. The longer the circuit, the more challenging the run. Cross-country skiing requires a certain amount of stamina even for a 3 km run.

You have a choice of renting skis for half a day, a day, and up to an entire season. Some ski rentals allow you to purchase the pair of skis if after renting them you can't shake off the ski bug. Very enterprising of the Swiss to sell them at a second-hand price.

Like mountain skiing, cross-country skiers need a daily or a seasonal pass to go on the ski run. Night skiing is becoming more and more available, so for those who want to avoid the day crowds, here's your chance.

Sledding/Tobogganing

Santa Claus is often pictured as being a professional manoeuvring a sled, but be warned, these contraptions go pretty fast. Sleds are now available in bright plastics, most often seen with young children having the time of their lives going like the devil down the snow hill. There are sleds and toboggans for adults as well.

Snowboarding

Enough young high-schoolers are caught up with this sport to make snowboarding a teenage favourite. Gripping a board roughly the shape of a Häagen-Dazs lolly stick, you start at some boisterously high altitude (frequently on virgin snow) and snowboard your own

S's down the mountain. Strictly for those who already know how to ski and how to fall correctly. Davos in the canton of Graubünden (Grisons) and Leysin in Vaud are two top spots for snowboarding fans.

Skikjöring

Whether you are a spectator or a participant, skikjöring is a lesser-known type of skiing on a flat slope or frozen lake behind a galloping horse. You'll love trying this, but wear protection against the tiny ice chips that tend to fly into your eyes.

Hiking (G: Wanderweg)

Switzerland can boast of 50,000 km of pure calf-toning delight for hiking, the least expensive sports option. Yellow signs indicate the amount of time you will take to your next destination, giving you an idea of how long you'll be away. Anti-skiers can enjoy blissful hours away from the slopes. One bit of advice: never go off the hiking trail and do let one other person know the direction you are taking.

Curling

They say curling is to the Swiss what pétanque is to the French. Curling is not a sport for sissies but it's not the choice of grand slalomers either. A heavy granite curling stone shaped like a kettle is thrown in slow motion towards the targeted spot. Good fun for those with a strong back and preferably not pregnant.

Other types of spectator sports include polo on ice, dog racing, bobsledding, ice-skating, ice hockey, monoskiing, ski marathon, skibobbing and the very famous hot-air ballooning in Chateau-d'Oex.

Should the 2002 Winter Olympics be held in the Sion Valais/Wallis region, it would be best to change your itinerary before roofing up the ski rack onto your spacewagon. In any case, you would be wise to call up the tourist office in the resort of your choice to enquire if

The mountains, minty cool air and gratifying panorama all contribute to Saas Fee being a frequently visited resort.

there are any popular events held in that area. The last thing you want is to be left out in subhuman temperatures without a hotel room to call your own.

You can mingle with ski buffs and demigods among other gorgeously tanned Europeans and Americans in these perennially crowded resorts: Arosa, Crans-Montana, Davos, Engleberg, Grindelwald, Gstaad, Interlaken, Klosters, Saas Fee, St. Moritz, Verbier, Villars, Wengen and Zermatt.

SUMMER SPORTS
(June till end September)

Three months into the season of glorious golden sunshine and slow-moving steam boats did we gradually discover what Ernest Hemmingway and Noel Coward had known for decades – one summer on the Swiss Riviera and you would want to invest in a 5-room chalet overlooking the placid Lake Leman. If Keats had to compare summer to nature's fruits, it might be clusters of succulent Riesling-Sylvaners, the Swissified grape christened by the Swiss scientist Müller from Thurgau. Drink in the intoxicating breeze and the blended smells of ripening garden fruits, then decide for yourself at which chalet upon which hill you will hang your name plate.

Summer hosts a massive variety of activities as endless as the number of rocky windswept trails. No time to light the barbecue; it's a packed lunch and off you'll go:

Walking / Hiking / Jogging / Mountain-climbing

Listed according to the degree of difficulty, your legs would be the best vehicle to carry you to the sights, smells, sounds and salubrity of nature's homegrown leisure pursuits. Never much of a hiker myself, I mused over the fact that it truly isn't the distance which made hiking disagreeable. With the right company and the right equipment (comfortable hiking boots a must), you can basically scale any mountain.

Think of Switzerland as one long journey into recovering from the throes of this toxic world. Carry a light lunch, extra fruit bars, drinking water, a lightweight hooded jacket, a hiking map (if you intend to go where few have gone) and a practical Swiss army knife. Check the weather forecast the day before setting off (tel: 162). Rain can be a nuisance, especially when you are not prepared to be soaked.

Some of the best and most breathtaking vistas can be viewed at eagle-eye altitudes from summits around Lucerne, the Bernese Oberland sections and the Jungfrau region.

Swimming

Landlocked with its water positively tasteless, swimming in the lake can be as private as bathing in your own tub the size of an Olympic pool. Definitely recommended for family-oriented types, swimming in the lake promises to be one activity you would look forward to every weekend.

With the vast number of lakes in Switzerland open all year for swimming aficionados (1,500 lakes, give or take a dozen more or less), it's no surprise indoor pools are pretty quiet by comparison.

It is assuredly worth the effort to get to your destination early. It would appear as if everyone had the same bright idea to spend the lazy Saturday on a crocodile float, Chablis in hand and veal sausages smoking on an outdoor grill.

Boating / Canoeing / Rowing / Yachting / River Rafting

There's nothing quite like the pace of a wooden rowboat bobbing unostentatiously, almost indifferently to the maddened whizzing of cars along the autoroutes. Lake Gruyère, Neuchâtel, Thunersee, Brienz See, Lake Constance, Lake Lugano, and of course the four branches of lakes in the Lucerne area. All giants in promoting watersports and summer events.

Many have taken the opportunity to hire a camper and drive to the campsite on Friday evening so that by early Saturday morning, after a solid müesli breakfast, everyone is already in their paddle boats in the middle of the lake. There are various kinds of lake-faring floatables for hire by the hour or by the day including canoes, paddle boats, motor boats, and kayaks.

Horseback Riding / Equestrian Circuits

Riding is a splendid way to chat up a girlfriend or ask the boss for a raise but more importantly it is both fun and thrilling. Though it can be expensive and a possible pain in the behind, this is one activity that can transport you back to the time of Chaucer or Hardy.

This sport is well developed in Alsace and in the Jura region. Also in Le Puy-en-Velay, where living on a farm can be an unforgettable experience.

Minigolf

The merry game of potting the ball into the hole can also be the winding down of a day well spent by the lake. Introduced by our friend, the only snag to this game is the embarrassment caused by children giggling at you for missing the hole. Again.

Parashooting / Hang-gliding / Bungee-jumping

If the last five suggestions haven't given you the impetus to leap out of your pyjamas into your leotards, then you are truly the Mel Gibson type of sportsman/woman. Looking to dive off a precipice or fighting acrophobia in a hot-air balloon? It will cost you Sfr. 150 to bungee-jump in Titlis, but what does it matter when you have decided to freefall several *hundred* metres? We were surprised every summer by the number of people who thought they could outdo old Mel. Not advisable for children under 16, adults over 55 doing it for the first time, or anyone with a heart condition.

The Urmiberg valley in Brunnen, Titlis in Engelberg or the Gorge of the Inn (Scoul) are last resorts for those easily bored.

Bicycling

If you don't own a bike, you can easily rent one from the larger train stations. After more than 700 years of trying to get it right, health-conscious Swiss have succeeded in creating a labyrinth of biking trails that will make you want to buy your own racer. An amusing sport for all, especially those prone to imitate professional bikers during the annual *Tour de France*.

Tennis / Badminton / Table-tennis

Tennis fever reaches a boiling peak during summer when Eurosport channel televises live the tournaments from around the world. The most popular of ball games, tennis courts are the most difficult to rent unless you are a member of a club.

Try to locate summer discount coupons in your mailbox alongside all the junkmail, or ask a friend or colleague to recommend you some good facilities.

CLINICAL LIVING

It couldn't be a coincidence that the World Health Organisation is headquartered in Geneva, could it? Their standard of operation would have to reflect the model country they have chosen as their base. Clean, healthy and happy living can be achieved not by wishing for it but working for it.

By the turn of the 19th century, royalty from the grand houses of Battenberg and Austria began faithful pilgrimages to convalesce in Switzerland. Today, the bejewelled hundreds from the Taiwanese to the Turkish come with the same intention. The Swiss have carved an imposing reputation for themselves during the periods of industrialisation and the two world wars. They had invested in the most sought-after elixir of life – health and happiness.

When the husband and I lived in Clarens, in the canton of Vaud, we would spend endless summer weekends on our balcony with a tray of biscuits, spying on loaded sheiks. Before I write myself into a

The garden of the Clinique de la Prairie and our exceptionally good view of any on-goings around the fountain.

lawsuit, let me clarify why. Right across from our home sits the Clinique de la Prairie, a spa-cum-clinique of no shallow repute. A closely guarded, beautifully manicured garden attracts its wealthy clientele to sit on their deckchairs in the afternoon sun. It would seem that these corpulent businessmen and their wives have entered the sanctum sanctorum of salubrity. They come to revitalise, rejuvenate and repose under very close and subservient supervision.

No one denies the fact that the Swiss talk candidly about their *slight* mania for cleanliness and healthy living. If you grew up with the aphorism "If you don't live healthily, you live in hell" – well, it's difficult to live otherwise.

Switzerland has the highest ratio of doctors to patients in the world. There is one physician to every 654 inhabitants in urban areas. In rural areas, there is an average of one doctor to every 1,000. This is an extraordinarily high ratio, but small wonder considering the many state-owned and private hospitals in Switzerland.

Hot Springs

I have to thank the Harbaugh family for bringing to my attention the hot springs in Switzerland. Pockets of these natural baths all over the country draw foreigners like ants to an open picnic basket. Leukerbad (1,415 m), Yverdon-les-bains and the Caumausee in Flims (1,127 m) have pools of naturally health-sustaining waters (or so history recounts), which are visited by thousands yearly. Their waters are a skin-peeling 44°C, and winter seems a hazardously wicked season to go. How healthy can it be when you come out lobster red to catch your death of pneumonia in –5° cold? The young and the old, the frail and the frolicsome – they still go and they do return. The food at the spas is usually good and through much trial and testing, deemed the most nutritious.

Fancy a lymphatic draining session? How about soaking in a Turkish bath while you do your facial peeling? Such cures are popular in hole-in-the-wall places like Flumserberg and St. Moritz in Graubünden. Who knows? Perhaps Friedrich Nietzsche wrote *Thus Spake Zarathustra* while having a subaquatic massage in Sils-Baselgia near St. Moritz. But no worries. A thousand-odd franc revitalise-yourself package is supposed to melt away your secular worries, including unwanted stress and cellulitis. That is, if spending the money hasn't put you into hysterics already.

Chapter Six

EDUCATION: PUBLIC, PRIVATE, AND THE VERY PRIVATE

The Swiss educational system is hardly ever used in the singular sense because more than one system is employed. Some speculate that there may be as many as 26 systems, perhaps because 26 cantons make up Switzerland – they rarely follow a state-introduced system nor will they comply with one owing to the complexity of the cantons and the requirements of local authorities.

This is also why you may not appeal to a ministry of education. They haven't got one. If you have a teenager on your hands, or a pre-schooler, the canton you're registered at as the one you are residing in will be the canton in charge of educating, financing and in general plotting your child's future career.

We have had the misfortune of hearing one sob story too many from expatriate parents who suffered from the lack of federal coordination. Since each canton determines its own system of elementary, secondary and tertiary education, when families have to move to another canton, it is inevitably the school-going children who have to endure the most changes. The types of schools and designations for them are markedly different from region to region and from canton to canton, right down to the number of compulsory schooling and days in the school calendar.

An Irish woman I befriended told me the woes of settling in the canton of her husband's choice without giving a second thought to her two adolescents' education. Over coffee, she tearfully confided that their education have been at best as well-guided as the railroad tracks. That wasn't so bad, I thought foolishly to myself.

Not if they are so set that that's the only way they will go, she said resignedly.

Swiss children spend more time in school compared to children in neighbouring countries, a gruelling 40 hours a week in some schools. This goes on for a good part of their adolescence, eight to nine years in all.

Ninety-five percent of all students attend a cantonal or communal school. Swiss schools, if you are bent on sending your child to one, are public and attendance is strict and mandatory. Truancy is very low since teachers double up as military officers on the prowl for students going AWOL. Even if you are a discerning parent who has an excellent reason for requesting early dismissal for your child near the end of the term, you have a 50–50 chance of having your request denied.

Switzerland spends approximately 14.5 billion Swiss francs on education and research, no extravagant sum for a country hellbent on pursuing academic excellence *par excellence*. There are those who complain that the educational system is too selective, streaming the low achievers to the point of no transfer. Potential late bloomers who did not excel early enough are given little opportunity to do so later.

There are over 400 private educational establishments, half of which are supported by the National Federation. While Geneva and Zurich claim the most pupils, boarding schools are concentrated in the French-speaking parts of Switzerland and represent no less than 50 nationalities.

A Note to All Expatriates

The point cannot be overemphasised: different cantons operate differently because the Swiss constitution assigns the main responsibility to the cantons, which shares it with the communes. The 1972 national referendum to make education a joint responsibility of the Confederation and the cantons was rejected.

Before you cart your children off to school, have a talk with the school principal or director. If you are inflexible as to home leave or dates of departing to your home country, discuss this with the person in charge. Different cantons do have different school calendars, and once you've sent them off to a local public school, you can expect tedious delays in transferring them to another.

FROM KINDERGARTEN TO PRIMARY SCHOOL

As a rule, kindergarten is a more viable option than leaving petite Patricia at home with the au pair. The Swiss nursery is a magical arena where the teachers teach these little fidgeties to finger-paint, write and spell duosyllabic words. After a period of two to three years, depending on the age of your dumpling, he or she will enter compulsory primary school. If there is one thing the cantons can agree on wholeheartedly it is that basic and fundamental schooling is of pivotal importance in the development of the child's intellect.

In the early days, education throughout much of Europe was in the hands of the church and the ability to read and write was a privilege reserved for the very wealthy elite. It was during the Reformation (1523–28) and the Counter Reformation (1548–86) that the need for expanding elementary education came into being. The Swiss educational system advanced further under the influence of 18th century philosopher and writer Jean-Jacques Rousseau (1712–78) and Zurichois educationist Johann Heinrich Pestalozzi (1746–1827).

Today's primary schoolchild can attend the public school either in the village or in the city for free. If the parents have enough money to burn, private boarding or finishing school is a feasible alternative.

Whether school is in the morning or afternoon session, you can entrust your child for six days in a week to be drilled in the rudiments of native language, music and art, arithmetic, local history and geography, physical education, and nature study.

In a 1962 comparative essay by American Admiral Hyman Rickover entitled "Swiss Schools and ours: Why theirs are better", he extols the Swiss system of better teaching, longer school days and school year as being the key to better-schooled children. Perhaps he was stationed in several institutions where the children had displayed such aptitude.

Clearly, closer to the 21st century, the brunt of responsibility has been displaced. Standardised curricula and parental responsibility to act as teachers outside the classroom are latter-day traditions that have proved useful if not somewhat inconvenient to working parents.

If you have children who are in a public school, your responsibility to teach has not diminished just because Junior and his sister trot off to school with a satchel twice their size on their backs. If Junior fails miserably in a subject, you will likely be called up and interrogated as to how much time you have been spending with him.

UPPER MIDDLE SCHOOL OR GYMNASIUM

After compulsory education, Jean-Pierre Secondaire should be at an age where most parents develop migraines and deep-seated regrets of having conceived that child 14 or 15 years ago. Be it as it may, he would have graduated from primary to upper middle school. It is said that the occupations of the Swiss are chosen prior to their 16th birthday, usually after the onset of exam fever and pressure to keep up with the Baumgartners' computer-hack prodigy.

By this time, Jean-Pierre Secondaire's structured course will lead him from age 16 to 19 to sit an examination called *Maturité* in order to apply for tertiary education in a university. Should Jean-Pierre fail to obtain any one of the eleven *Maturité* certificates, he will be obliged to serve an apprenticeship for a period of 2 to 4 years, after which he may further his education by attending evening classes in General Studies.

UNIVERSITY

Switzerland has ten tertiary institutions, five of them in the Swiss-German part of the country. They are:

1. University of Basel (founded in 1460)
2. University of Bern (1834)
3. University of Zurich (1833)
4. Swiss Federal College of Technology, Zurich (1855) and
5. St. Gallen Graduate School of Economics (1899)

    The other five are in Swiss-Romande parts. They are:

1. University of Geneva (1873)
2. University of Lausanne (1890)
3. University of Neuchâtel (1909)
4. University of Fribourg (1889) and
5. Swiss Federal Institute of Technology, Lausanne (1890).

A university education lasts anything from five to seven years; more commonly seven than five, unless we are talking child prodigy here. Higher education is the responsibility of the cantons as well, with the exception of the Federal College of Technology in Zurich (ETHZ) and the Federal Institute of Technology in Lausanne (EPFL).

Going to university is assuredly not for the halfhearted, faint-hearted, or the soft-headed. At the ripe old age of 20, the Swiss have

*Affectionately called 'La banane' – the banana – because of its crescent shape,
this library at the University of Lausanne is only one of several on campus.*

to decide at which institution of the ten listed above they want to spend
much of their effort, time, and money. In the 1989–90 school year,
only 16% of 20- to 24-year-olds were university students.

Women students enrolled are on the rise. Compared to the
unliberated 1960s, when only 20% of the student population were
women, the enrolment of 38% in the late 1980s shows that women in
Switzerland are gradually warming up their laptops instead of their
stovetops.

Over the years we befriended students from various universities,
and one of the things we discovered was that the number of applicants
far outnumber the places available in universities. Therefore the
entrance exams are cruelly difficult to pass and only a small percentage of students are accepted into the faculty of their choice. This has
been a moot topic for decades in spite of Swiss campuses being so
inordinately huge and impressive.

Out of the 19 German-speaking cantons, about 20,690 attend the
University of Zurich, 9,500 the University of Bern, and 6,800 the

University of Basel. In the six French-speaking cantons, where there are four universities, Geneva has 12,000 students, Lausanne approximately 7,000, Fribourg 5,800 and Neuchâtel 2,500.

To many Swiss and resident expatriates, sending their pre-adults off to university can be a discouraging experience. Those still bent on beating the system may have to change their course of choice to something completely different.

In *Der Bund,* Berne daily newspapers, Zurich's local government has decided to make English a requisite subject for students in the upper classes, beginning in October 1999 – replacing French as the first foreign language to be taught. Good business sense? Bad cultural setback? Interesting debates ensue.

Restrictive sizes of Swiss tertiary institutions notwithstanding, 55 million Swiss francs have been generously poured into creating an informatics network linking all the universities, polytechnics and research centres. Education is a serious business: not only does it generate international trade, it is seen to be the right of every individual. This explains the high percentage of literacy and the escalating standard of living.

There are no private universities in Switzerland other than the Theological Faculty in Lucerne, founded in 1878.

THE VERY PRIVATE SCHOOLS

Switzerland has 350 private and boarding schools, one of which I had the good fortune of visiting. The English headmaster of a very private school once asked me to tea (it turned out to be a glass of sherry) in his study; I was then his neighbour and hoping to find a part-time teaching job.

Stealthily perched on a hillside, this venerable co-ed school had the task of moulding well-behaved and intellectually stimulated minds. The porch, surrounded by a cluster of firs, leads one to an oak door of stately proportions.

The headmaster of Hill House is a gentleman with an idée fixe that educating his 12- and 13-year-olds takes more than confinement to a classroom, book in hand and an ominous-looking paddle in the other. The general aura surrounding the darkened panels behind 18th century drawings of croquet in session screams order and achievement. Floorboards creaked and doors squeaked in the building which housed no more than 60 schoolchildren. I viewed the premises with a kind of awkward amazement and sympathised with the parents who desire this kind of education but cannot afford it. The headmaster assured me that this private boarding school is *not* inexpensive. The squirrels could have told me that.

Pick up the *International Herald Tribune* and there in the education classifieds will be establishments much like Hill House seeking adolescents to impart their special knowledge. Private schools are generally small and the ratio of teacher to students kept comfortably low.

Many are fond of singing their praises about the way these private schools teach their children. Their curriculum is different from that in the Swiss public school; English boarding schools follow the English curriculum and American private schools follow the American one. This facilitates the home-returning process especially if you intend to stay in Switzerland for no more than two years.

HOTEL SCHOOLS AND VOCATIONAL INSTITUTES

With so many 5-star hotels in Switzerland, one would expect as many 5-star chefs and staff to run them. The booming tourist industry has paved the way for many foreign investors in this field of education. International emblems and a host of flags grace the campuses of these schools.

As I mentioned previously, Switzerland is a cornucopia of races and the breeding ground of internationalists. To cater to the wants and whims of tourists who flock there by the millions, its hotel industry has got to be topnotch.

Take the Hotel Management School in Les Roche in Crans-Montana. Ask Elizabeth Taylor or Princess Stephanie if they've encountered problems settling in for a fortnight in that very expensive ski resort region. Other international bigwigs, including the Institut Hotelier Cesar Ritz in Le Bouveret, the Hotel and Tourism School in Leysin and the Hotel Institut in Montreux, recruit students from every continent. The English-speaking students you may encounter in a restaurant serving you baked rabbit could well be a second-year student doing six months of practical training.

We remember fondly three-hour evening meals in the company of such students talking about ways of currying chicken or finding Asian shops selling tapioca starch or *wanton* skins. This is an excellent opportunity to gather information about the availability of foods otherwise unheard of in your corner of Switzerland.

The Swiss government takes its cue from demand. If there is a strong demand for certain vocations, chances are funding will follow and institutes will come into existence. Dentistry, languages, design and business are some of the more predominant career options.

Now more than ever, the establishment of adult education institutions for parental training, correspondence courses, university entrance programmes and night schools are attracting older people who want to better themselves instead of rusting away like barn hinges into premature oblivion. Adult education courses are found in the *Migros Klubschule*, founded in 1944 and located in every canton. To date, there are at least 50 *Migros Klubschule* centres offering courses in languages, leisure activities such as cooking and photography, training and continuing higher education to more than 500,000 participants.

Some sophisticated (but getting more common every May) holiday packages might even include a summer stint in one of the many language institutes. Some Europeans are already trilingual, and brushing up on their third language during vacation time may seem a little unnecessary, but for a couple of hours a day, I was surprised to find how far one can improve conversationally and grammatically.

Live and learn – whyever not?

DO'S, DON'TS AND DUNNOS

To be faced with a dubious eyeball-rolling response from a native Swiss can be an unnerving experience. It should not be something to be inured to because once the ice is broken, you will find the Swiss to be loyal-to-death comrades. The cursory glance from the butcher, baker, or candlestick maker is symptomatic of anyone who has ever dealt with foreigners. And let's face it – Switzerland is saturated with foreigners.

As you increase awareness of your own preconceptions and stereotypes of Swiss culture, you will eventually build an understanding and rapport that could easily last you a lifetime. This chapter is geared to help you cope with the stress of simply not knowing what to expect, with some personal ideas and hints on how to react when faced with transitional chaos.

Attending a Baptism

By and large, infant or child baptisms are still carried out in churches irrespective of whether the parents are practising Christians. When you are invited to a baptism, it helps to know that it is an outward and public declaration that the child is being inducted into the community of the church. Normally the ritual does not take more than half an hour. In many places, guests are treated to a four- or five-course meal and a proper invitation is sent to announce the occasion.

Do bring a present for the child or baby. An appropriate gift could be an illustrated Bible, especially if you want to give a meaningful gift that can be cherished for many years.

Attending a Funeral

Funerals can be the most uncomfortable gatherings. Contrarily, it can also be the most moving. This is one occasion where to be late shows great disrespect. The meal after the service, called the funeral feast, is aimed at pooling the relatives and friends together to help bear the grief better. During this time, it is customary to offer your condolences to family members you know.

Do wear dark clothes, preferably black, to the funeral. If you have children, and have to bring them along, try to restrict their movements during the service.

Do send letters of sympathy if you feel uncomfortable about going personally to the funeral service or to the wake.

At Museums

Do ask if they allow photography in the museum. Seeing them rip out your film is a bitter and unnecessary experience.

Auto Newspaper Vending Machines

Do pay the exact amount. These vending machines are easy targets for private detectives bent on slapping a hefty Sfr. 50 fine on newspaper pirates.

Bargain-hunting

Do wait for the two yearly sale events in January and in July. Large discounts (up to 70%) and frenzied grabbing make the six-month interim worthwhile.

Charity Canvassers at Your Door

Dunno is the best way to get out of this situation. Since we lived in a prominent residential block, being accosted once every week became a stickler in my craw. This is a good time to revert back to your mother tongue (if it's some exotic language) to keep them at bay. Alternatively, **don't** answer the door, though this is the cowardly way of dealing with such people.

Concierge Responsibilities

Do pester your concierge if the washing machines don't work properly, if the corridors are dirty or if there is anything else amiss with the orderliness of the building.

Dried Foodstuff

Do ask family members to send whatever you require especially if the ingredients are indigenous, or available only in your home country.

If your package comes through the post, normally you wouldn't have too many difficulties. When my parents-in-law came to visit

Out of all the soup-brewing ingredients displayed in this photo, only the whole almonds can be bought in Chinese speciality shops. If there are certain types of food you cannot live without, bring them along with you.

bearing gifts of much needed potato flour in order for me to make steamed pumpkin cake, the customs officer didn't bat an eyelid. It could be that they had honest faces or simply the fact that no matter how much potato flour resembles heroin, it's *still* potato flour.

Drinking Water
Don't forget to get rid of the calque (mineral deposits) in your kettle or boiler if you have one. Unless you filter the water, you should decalcify your heating appliances once a week with undiluted vinegar.

Don't go lapping up natural stream water when hiking. Tap water is generally safe but if you are new in Switzerland, bottled mineral water or boiled water is advisable for the first few days. Water from fountains is generally unsafe; it is more for animal consumption.

Driving ...

Do have all your papers ready and in order. This means: your car permit, your driver's licence, insurance papers, papers documenting details of previous accidents, the sticker to go on the motorway (called a *vignette*), and a green antipollution sticker that tells you when you need to go for the next smog check.

Do check that your headlights and tail lights are working. The police will stop you for faulty lights.

Don't honk unnecessarily. More often than not, drivers flash their headlights once or twice if a) you are hogging the fast lane, b) you are doing something illegal, c) they wish to stop for a hitchhiker, or d) there is danger ahead.

Driving Under the Influence

Don't. Don't and don't. The BAC (blood alcohol content) limit is at a tough 0.08%. The worst thing to happen is imprisonment. Nothing good can come out of this one.

Farmers' Markets

Don't pick at the produce or finger them excessively if you don't plan to purchase any. Most of the locally produced fruits and vegetables sold at these open-air markets are remarkably fresh, though they can be a wee bit more expensive than at Migros, the supermarket chain.

Feeding the Birds

Do keep stale baguettes to feed those feathery friends by the lake.

Stale breads are a feast to the lake's wildlife especially during the cold and wet months of October through February.

Friends

Don't hit on the pretty Swiss girls with all your savage, primeval charm without first understanding who her parents are or what they do for a living. The Swiss are still highly conservative and any kind of flair is equivalent to a lot of hot air if respect is not shown to the

Switzerland is the melting pot of internationalism. Students represent nationalities from Finland, the Bahamas, Taiwan, Pakistan, South Africa and Singapore. If you are gregarious, you will find yourself a part of a mini United Nations of friends before the end of your term in Switzerland.

parents. **Do** listen and observe. More is accomplished this way if you want to understand what makes the Swiss tick.

Greetings and Salutations

The Swiss greet each other by gently grazing cheek to cheek three times. If you have just been introduced, a firm handshake will be offered, especially if you are obviously non-European. However, first-time cheek grazing is not unheard of. When they part company, they 'kiss' each other goodbye in the same manner.

The Swiss are very sensitive and sensible people. They will stick to handshakes if they sense embarrassment or discomfort.

When you enter the store, the hairdresser's, or any other establishment, you would be pleasantly greeted with a *Bonjour*, *Guten tag*, or *Buon giorno*. In Switzerland, greeting each other is a polite tradition which has survived many centuries. Leaving the store, paying at the cashier, or quitting the office, one is courteously wished "Goodbye" or "Have a nice day." Many European countries promote and encourage habitual greetings, and the Swiss practise it diligently.

The Swiss are also fond of greeting each other with an informal *Salut!* irrespective of their locality of origin. For goodbye, the Italian *Ciao!* is used.

You will learn as you go along that the Swiss, although apparently strict and isolating at first, are actually very accommodating people. They may be shy at first. Think of them as being quiet folk who simply want to live their gracious lives without much fuss.

Grocery Shopping

Do bring your own canvas or plastic bags or canvas trolleys to do your grocery shopping. Paper or plastic bags cost Sfr. 0.30 at the supermarket. Alternatively you can use the empty boxes available in some stores to cart your groceries home.

Don't go into the supermarket between 5:30 and 6:30 pm if you can help it. At this rush hour anything fresh is bound to have been sold.

Grocery Shopping across the Border

Dunno works once or twice if you are new to the country and therefore unfamiliar with the customs. Many go to France to purchase their groceries but at the entry points Swiss police will make spot checks to see if you have over-purchased the limited amounts allowed of meat, dairy products and liquor. You are advised to ask for the list of tax-free goods at the customs before stocking up for the week.

Hitching a Ride

Do hitch a ride safely by thumbing a sign near a convenient spot where vehicles have room to pull out.

Don't hitch a ride near the autoroute entrances or exits. This is not only unlawful; it is dangerous.

Joking about the War

Don't joke about World War II or related events you found hilarious in your home country. Some wounds run deep, even after a generation of healing.

Although the Swiss remained neutral in World War II, one has to remember they were not isolated from the devastating effects of the war. Almost everyone had someone dear to them who was involved in the war. Anxiety for relatives living across borders only increased tension as the war progressed.

Legal Advice

Do take legal action or advice against rental sharks or when you are involved in an accident which calls for a good defence lawyer.

Noisy Neighbours

Do alert the concierge if your neighbour insists on moving heavy furniture or having a noisy party after 10 pm. Noise and nonsense after that sacred hour is not tolerated. If your concierge is indifferent or unhelpful, call the police.

Old Clothes, Shoes, Bags, Furniture ...

Do keep any unwantables or unwearables for charitable organisations. There is at least one day in the month when a large truck comes by to pick up bulky furniture; there may also be junk collectors who want to relieve you of your stuff.

Parking Fines

Blue parking zones (*Zone bleue / Blaue zone / Zona blu*) are marked by blue lines on the ground and allow you a maximum of one and a half hours' free parking. The red parking zones (*Zone rouge / Rote zone / Zona rota*) allow 15 hours of free parking. You have to display the parking disc to show the time of arrival. You can ask your bank for these parking discs or purchase one in the Migros or stationery store.

The white parking zones are pay-parking areas where the automatic metermaids stick out like sore thumbs, or there's an auto-pay machine nearby. Only if neither is in sight do you take it to be free parking.

One very unusual characteristic of parking cars in Switzerland is their candid way of heaving one half of the vehicle onto the raised pavement. You could have enough space for the vehicle to park within the given area but they insist on leaping onto pedestrian territory. Since I am no mechanic, I cannot say what damage this might cause to your suspension, to say nothing about your axle and alignments. The only probable reason is that they don't want to hog the road space as this can be awfully wanting, especially in smaller towns where the roads are dangerously narrow. This is one instance where when in Switzerland, I won't do as the Swiss do.

Dunno is one way of weaselling out of a fine if you are caught a few minutes after the time allowed in the blue zones. Accompanying it with a "Sorry" and "I'll be more careful next time" usually saves you from paying Sfr. 30.

Do pay up at the parcometer car parks. Charges vary depending on location – whether closer to shops and amenities. The Swiss ticketing police are normally there, come rain, shine, hail or snow.

Paying Your Fines

Do pay up all your parking fines. The Swiss computerised system at all border patrols are frequently updated and are very efficient in locating the culprits. You can pay your fines through the Post.

Pet Peeves

Do get your pet vaccinated and papers of ownership in order before agreeing to keep frisky Fifi. Check with the apartment renting agency if animals are allowed in your building.

Do put your dog on a leash, or if you prefer not to, make sure it responds well to your voice commands.

Do use the black plastic bags rolled up in green dispensary metal bins along the road to retrieve any poo left by your pet in public places.

Picking Flowers

Don't vandalise by picking the lovely flowers hand-planted by the army of gardeners responsible for beautifying the Swiss landscape. Many wild flowers, especially in the lower and upper Alps are protected and should NOT be picked.

Picking Fruits

Don't trespass on private property and don't go picking fruit behind fences.

Picking off the Grapevine

Do take the time to indulge in some back-strengthening exercise and earn some money at the same time. For about Sfr. 100 a day, you can slip into the skin of a grape harvester and enjoy picking these clusters of wine fruit. Your meals are most likely provided because you will be spending at least ten hours in the invigorating, fresh, wholesome, cool air. The catch is, even when it rains, you will still be a-harvesting in the invigorating, fresh, wholesome, cool air.

Public Toilets

Do bring your little ones to public toilets as opposed to bringing them by a large grove of pines or by a small stream. Most people will be happy to oblige you at the gas stations. Some public toilets require a Sfr. 0.20 payment, others at train stations charge Sfr. 1, but by and large, they are free and very well maintained.

Queuing Up

Don't jump the queue at the PTTs, banks, supermarket cashiers, ticketing outlets or anywhere else, unless glares and malicious snorts make your day…

Recycling

Do try to recycle all your recyclables. You won't get a trophy but you will be contributing to conserving the Swiss landscape.

Stamps on Your Letters

Do put sufficient stamps on your letters. See cost of postage in Chapter Three. The PTT will send you an advice slip if you have underpaid, and you will then have to go to the area PTT office to pay the balance.

Swearing

Don't. This is neither necessary nor pleasant. Switzerland is still regarded as a religious country with a much stricter moral standard than many other industrialised European countries.

Tipping

Do tip when you feel generous, even though the service tax is normally included in the bill. The newly implemented TVA (similar to the value added tax in the UK) is currently from 2.3–7.5%, so anything you purchase or whatever service you employ will include this.

Traffic Jams on the Motorway

Do find alternative routes home if you hate traffic jams. Nearer larger cities, the motorways start bottlenecking as early as 5 pm.

Trains...

Don't be tempted to steal into the first class carriage if you have a second class ticket. The scene if you are caught is guaranteed to be very humiliating and not worth the risk.

Do be careful with your money especially if you tend to nod off on trains.

Vocabulary for the Genteel Foreigner

Do practise a few basic words to make yourself understood. There are enough language books in Switzerland to put you in the poorhouse, but all you need is one which you feel comfortable with.

Volunteer or Relief Work

Do approach an organisation for volunteer work if life in the slow lane is unacceptable. There are over 200 international organisations in Switzerland. The WHO (World Health Organisation), ECC (European Culture Centre), ICRC (International Committee of the Red Cross), the High Commissariat for Refugees and numerous voluntary organisations are based in Geneva. This is one way of meeting expatriates from other countries.

Weddings

Swiss weddings have a tendency to go on for the entire day right through the night. There is often a lot of dancing and eating throughout the weekend. Church weddings occur after the couple are wed at the mayor's office or in the presence of a government representative.

Attending weddings in Switzerland can be a contagious pastime. Church weddings are more often than not romantic to the point of

being quixotic. Weddings are still the most important festive occasion in the eyes of most Swiss even though the number of divorce cases is distressingly high (33% or one in three marriages ends in divorce). The surveys done on Swiss marriages say women sashay down the aisle on average over the age of 27, while men give up bachelorhood at 29. Experts report over 2.2 billion Swiss francs being spent on weddings and setting up bridal households.

Do purchase something for the new couple's home. Household items are by far the most popular gifts. One simply cannot go wrong buying Bohemian crystal vases or Wedgwood teacups, unless you know beforehand the couple is into Alessi designer toothbrushes or condiment receptacles. See Chapter Three under 'Shopping' for places to go.

Basically, one couple's dream house is another's nightmare. If you know the couple, it's wiser to tap their brains as to what they would like for their wedding present. It is rare to present the couple with cash, but gift vouchers are becoming more common.

Do honk your car horn if you notice a train of cars following the bridal Rolls or carriage. This is one of the rare occasions to use your car horn: for a lovely tradition when everybody honks in acknowledgement of the happy event. Noisy, but *nice*.

Chapter Eight

ONE-DAY EXCURSIONS TO SOMEWHERE ELSE

The centrality of Switzerland lends itself marvellously to weekend excursions. The provincial joke that looking out the window in the morning had been banned because there wouldn't be anything left to do in the afternoon might be a bit overdone. I venture to suggest that all who live in Switzerland and who work, spend their Friday afternoons quietly meditating on where to go the coming weekend.

The Swiss adore travel, and like the sparrows, flutter off to some exotic location in search of new experiences. Come every summer, great masses of Swiss migrate across the borders.

As we were mostly surrounded by foreigners with a murderous curiosity to discover the undiscovered, our latter-day preoccupations gradually succumbed to similar whims. Our Canadian friend Carina from Montreal had such a nasty bite from the travel bug that staying in her apartment was tantamount to torture. Come Thursday evening and she would begin charting out a strategic, complex game plan to spend every waking moment of her weekend actively pursuing some leisure activity – for example, biking up a 20% gradient hill in search of a lake no one visits any more.

One-day Excursions to Somewhere Else is dedicated to those Carinas in the world – in love with adventure and who jump into the deep end of the lake head first. Such excursions are stupendous fun especially if you go with good friends or a partner. If you are a parent brave enough to go with your entire brood of six or seven, having theme outings can be challenging: viewing castles in the vicinity or

Viewing this castle took only 20 seconds as this one-day sojourn was to the Swiss Vapeur Parc in le Bouveret, where miniature buildings and monuments can be seen from a moving miniature steam-engine.

locating interesting churches (Le Corbusier designed one in nearby Ronchamp in France) can be educational and relatively inexpensive. Rafting down famous rivers (not for the timid) and trying out new camping grounds can be a lot more titillating than staying at dormitories at the usual youth hostels.

Listed below are some ways of refreshing your romance with your spouse or simply knitting your family closer together, all the while exploring fascinating places in or within easy reach of Switzerland. Either way, you will develop that glassy look in the office or in class on Friday afternoons. But don't be embarrassed: you are not alone!

Going Underground

Organising a trip for international students to a brine reservoir in Bex was fun. Situated in a mountainside in the canton of Valais, the educational field trip on salt-mining begins with a short narrow-gauge train ride into this subterranean world of crystalised everyday salt. Other underground wonders include the St. Leonard underwater lake, supposedly the largest in Europe, and the St. Beatus Caves in Sundlauenen.

Down the Aare with a Paddle...

For Sfr. 70, you can canoe down the River Aare from Thun to Bern in three to four hours. Trips like this are guaranteed to give you sore arm muscles but a hog-wild chance of a lifetime to brave the elements. You can pick up numerous brochures at any train station with tourist information. River-rafting, sailing and canoeing are pleasant overtures to a symphony of delightful activities available throughout summer and autumn.

Evian Water for Free!

That little stretch of the French Nationale 5 (or N5) road from either Geneva or St. Gingolph is reminiscent of some forgotten era of the fifties when movies such as *Guerre des boutons* made cinema-goers teary-eyed with nostalgia. Careening around lazy bends from the opposite side of the lake, a carefree, almost winsome feeling takes over and raising the rooftop on one's convertible becomes every owner's prerogative.

Evian-les-bains is famous for its mineral water from the glacial Alps, which is bottled for millions around the world. From the frontier post at St. Gingolph, it takes approximately 30 minutes to reach Evian. From Geneva, it takes approximately 50. Many Valaisans (people from the canton of Valais) and Vaudois (people from the canton of Vaud) cross borders every weekend to do their grocery shopping in the mammoth-sized supermarket aptly called *Mammouth* (pronounced 'Mah-moot') a couple of kilometres outside Evian, just before Thonon-les-bains.

As a town, Evian is no Las Vegas: a posh casino does face Switzerland but there ends the similarity. The thermal baths draw the odd tourist or two during the off-peak season but people are usually content enough frolicking at the lake's edge. For a one-day visit, Evian may be a pleasant distraction. If you live anywhere along Lake Leman, you may want to shave 30–40% off your grocery bill by doing your supermarketing in the Centre Commercial.

For the frugal shopper who doesn't mind stocking enough Evian mineral water to take a bath in, there are two sources (common knowledge to locals) that spew this liquid gold generously for free from the road above the lake route. All you've got to do is bring your own twelve gallon container and a camera to prove it can be done!

Little Chalet on the Prairie

One day in the boondocks, in this case being the old parts of Emmental, in a horse-drawn carriage from Trachselwald to Grunen-matt, is a relaxing way to admire the scenic vista from the Jura mountains to the Alps.

Many who come to Switzerland have the shocking impression that fun and games are all they can think about. This was for me a gnawing feeling which proved to be true. Switzerland is very family-oriented and after *papa* and *maman* have spent many hours working their tails off during the week, it seems wholly justifiable to spend some well-earned money banished into the boondocks with the family.

This one-day excursion, drawn by two lovely Haflinger horses, won't make you rush back to the office in a hurry. It's the Swiss wild west version that should make this Somewhere Else something else.

Lyon in the West

Getting up at the crack of dawn to drive two hundred over kilometres to Lyon can be serious fun, but it's not for night owls who prefer to regale colourful stories at the pub the previous night … Short destination holidays are mood-lifters because leaving the old familiar routine can keep the adrenaline high until the next month-long vacation.

Lyon is France's second Paris. A fashionable city with certain theatrical fame, Lyon has over the years attracted Swiss day sojourners across the borders. Exploring unknown cities, especially those that can claim fortresses like the Notre Dame de Fourvière, and understanding their historical roots are fun endeavours for the children, if not equally so for adults who aren't history buffs. Nothing can be easier to budget if you are driving a clan of children with you. Prepare finger food lunches and you can snap the panoramic views as you picnic in resting areas along the autoroute.

The Oktoberfest in Munich

Heading up north, in the besotted footsteps of those who have chugged a pint or ten frothy *steins*, our next day excursion is to Germany's southern city of Munich. There Oktoberfest is celebrated for two weeks (ending the first Sunday in October) with gusto and a gallimaufry of vulgar antics, all in good fun.

In bawdy smoke-filled backrooms, Bavarian specialities like the *Spanferkel* (roasted suckling pig) and *Nurnberger Wurst* (little sau-

sages served from a barrel) make beer-chasing a lip-smacking fad.
During the last days of September, Swiss Germans and expatriates
make the journey for just one evening of bellying the beers.

It is a unique experience as beer gets spilled and sausages grilled
all over the 300 plus food outlets in downtown Marienplatz. Bring lots
of Deutschmarks and leave the children with the sitter.

Finespun Philately in Liechtenstein

Vaduz, the capital, is clearly marked by its castle, occupied by the
royal family of Prince Hans Adam, the reigning heir to Franz Joseph
II. A principality by no means unobstrusive, Liechtenstein is visited
by neighbouring Austrians, Germans and Swiss.

I found Liechtenstein to be compactly small, but with all the
trimmings of expertly glazed icing on the cake. You can visit this 157
sq. km constitutional empire via train to Buchs in the canton of St.
Gallen, or Sargens, taking the post bus into Vaduz. Best known for its
stamp designs, Liechtenstein has promoted itself as a stamp collec-
tor's paradise. You can and should view the homemade stamps from

1912 in the postage stamp museum (Städtle 37, Vaduz. Tel: 075-66259) or subscribe to the stamp issues in the Official Philatelic Service adjacent to the Post Office.

Lugano Here We Go!

The best thing about these one-day excursions is the undeniable fact that each one is bound to be more exciting than bowling and more impulsive than your last journey into the unknown. Lugano was one of my craziest ideas-turned-brilliant as the journey there took almost five hours (front wheel drive isn't the safest to crunch on snow), taking us through the Furkapass (2,440 metres) on a car-transporting train (travelling in a dark tunnel for ages), before landing us in suddenly sunny Lugano.

Lugano is the affluent Swiss Italian town sitting at the edge of Lago di Lugano (Lake Lugano). Nicknamed the 'Rio de Janeiro of the old world', it paints a picturesque canvas of lakeside serenity. The white sails of numerous yachts and catamarans dot shimmering aquamarine waters, urging one to jump into a swimsuit and into the 25°C waters.

On a late autumn's day, beckoned by the initial idea to get away from the routine humdrum of Saturday ennui, we sped eastward toward Aigle, then Brig, into the Furkapass, and south past Bellizona to Lugano. Ticino, as this region is called, belonged to Italy until 1512 and then belonged to the Swiss Confederation for 268 years before Napoleon rendered it a free canton. Later, it rejoined the Confederation and since then has become one of the most romantic cities travellers coming to Switzerland visit.

Lugano is a city of pedestrians; its climate is most suitable for taking long walks or bicycle rides to its many tourist attractions. The neoclassical town hall built in 1844, called the Municipio, is situated in the Piazza della Riforma, right in the heart of the city. From there, one can trod the much-beaten path to cathedrals San Lorenzo, Sta. Maria degli Angioli, Sant' Antonio and San Rocco. Those who would enjoy more than a perfunctory look into one of the world's best kept private galleries can head towards Castagnola to Pinacoteca Villa Favorita. Baron Heinrich von Thyssen's collection is no Guggenheim Museum, but art lovers flock there to see Van Eyck's *Annunciation*.

There is much to fall in love with in Lugano. The charm of Swiss Italian is very Italian; all big smiles and mama figures who love to tease. The old part of the city with its antiquated arcades has contemporary stores peddling anything from recycled papers to New Age health-preserving crystals. Here is where one can never be totally on one's guard. To expect the unexpected is the best preparation you'll have when you wind your way into this flavourful city of the South.

Milan by Any Name Still Smells the Same

All right, so the husband complains too much about your pizza – how bland it is, or how your anchovies are simply too salty, or how your Electrolux oven can't compare to an 18th century wood-burning stove, etc., etc. ... Think Milanese pizza and a short journey just to satisfy his tastebuds and your desire to buy an Armani dress.

Milan has the works: from La Scala, the music mecca of the opera, and the Duomo, a cathedral of such cosmic proportions you daren't enter without crossing yourself first, to the Pinacoteca de Brera ... to call this a place for art buffs is like calling Rome a medieval village. Travelling by car can be a tedious six hours if you live further north than Bern. Alternatively, you can spend the weekend there and return Sunday evening, having indulged in *spaghetti alle cozze e vongole* (spaghetti with clams and mussels) or *risotto con zucche e scampi* (rice with squash and shrimp).

When we did the one day stint to Milan, we discovered many super eateries and gelaterias featuring the obligatory Milanese dough and ice-cream. Shopping is an ancient and well known cure to boredom. As we crammed the trunk with hundreds of thousands of lira worth of goods, we were quite content with doggy-bagging a 12-inch pizza and two foaming cups of *ristretto* (coffee not for the

111

weak-stomached). As you wind your way back on the A4 and A5 *autostrada*, remember you will still need roughly 22,000 lira (Sfr. 32) for the toll fee to get through the Grand St. Bernard tunnel.

This was for us a proven method of living Italian. *Buono appetito!*

Capital Bern

Visiting the capital of any country is surely an educational trip. With seven kilometres of blister-causing shopping arcades, one should learn to leave one's American Express card at home. But seriously, Bern is more than boutiques and bear pits; the Houses of Parliament at Bundesplatz are not just a showy display of democracy. The Swiss are deeply proud of their government and the way it handles home policies.

No less than eleven 16th century historic fountains, beautifully painted and regularly cleaned, are situated along the main streets. Each fountain tells a quaint tale. The Ogre fountain is demonically gruesome: inspect it closely and you will discover an ogre snacking on a child. The Bernisches Historical Museum, Swiss Rifle Museum (*Schweizerisches Schutzenmuseum*) and the Einstein Museum are worth more than a cursory glance.

Located a stone's throw from the Einstein House is Einstein's World, a tiny shop founded by Charly Einstein, great grandson of the Nobel Prize winner. The shop at Kramgasse 5 is worth a look for strategic games and mind-bending tricks that will make short work of any Christmas shopping list.

The baroque Church of the Holy Ghost (1726–29) just outside the railway station is an excellent place to start wearing out your Adidas sneakers. From the medieval quarter of the city to the cobbled streets of expensive shops, you'll find that visiting the capital of Switzerland is a field trip you shouldn't miss.

Chapter Nine

FROM AARGAU CARROT CAKE TO ZURICH SLICED VEAL

Being Chinese, food comes very close to our hearts. In this shrinking world of mingled cultures, trying to find authentic cuisine is like needle-hunting in the Afghan desert. Swiss cuisine, often presumed nonexistent (or worse – to be French or German), has slowly regained sensational popularity in local inns and farmhouses. The answer to foreigners' outcry for something more than *rösti* and something less than fondue has indeed been found in the unlikeliest of places. In Swiss homes.

The early naive days of settling in a country where asparagus are white and cabbages purple certainly gave me kitchen nightmares – a degenerative kind of culture shock that renders the chef debilitatingly impotent in home cooking.

If Switzerland does not provide your familiar raw materials – in our case, sea fishes and everyday greens such as *kai lan* – the trick is to look for similar species. Westerners normally get along with what they can find in the supermarkets because the ingredients of their daily diet are not at polar extremes with foods found in Switzerland. When my husband had a yen for *laksa* (a local Singaporean spicy and creamy noodle dish), my first move to improvise was to call home for the dried ingredients. But sometimes one simply has to try new tastes, although deep in one's stomach, the gastric juices are pouring out for something that smacks of home.

The best way to sample authentic Swiss cooking is in someone's home. Our experiences in dining with Swiss friends in the comfort of their homes has been educational. A lot of their cooking takes a fair bit of preparation, marinating and simmering. However, the younger generation of Swiss has recipes which are simple to whip up without sacrificing taste. The hardworking executive need not eat at midnight for want of tasting sauerkraut the way *grand'maman* made it. (Those who wanted that would have asked *grand'maman* to make it in the first place.)

EATING IN VERSUS EATING AT THE INN

As you discover many out-of-the-way places that swear by their authenticity, you will also discover the high prices attached to each strand of half-melted cheese. Restaurants abound like squawking ducks in Lake Neuchâtel, but the kind of traditional cooking I look forward to is greatly limited.

Swiss foods and fads have lately undergone a new trend. With fast food chains and pop-it-in-the-microwave lunches undermining bistros and inns, the Swiss now have the choice of convenience over quality. High school and university students opt for convenience while traditionalists still make the trip home for lunch.

A simple lunch at MacDonald's will cost you roughly Sfr. 12–15. The Sfr. 5.60 Big Mac is the most expensive in the world. If you go to a Mövenpick restaurant, you'll be footing a bill for Sfr. 25–35 per person including a small 2 dl glass of wine. In a hotel restaurant, the bill can go up to Sfr. 35 and above if you prefer the à la carte to the noonday special. You can pay by cash or by card. Most restaurants will accept Visa, American Express, Eurocard, Diner's Club and Reka. These are usually advertised at the entrance or near the coat racks.

SO WHAT'S REALLY IN A SWISS MEAL?

There are many ingredients (surprise, surprise) and they are a colourful blend of sweets and salties. From the eastern canton of Graubünden, the paper-thin *Bündnerfleisch* is a marbled marvel of rump, air-dried and air-spiced over 1,800 m in that mountainous region. *Cornichons* (small pickles such as pickled gherkins) are side-chasers pickled to crunchy perfection. Add a glass of red *Veltliner* wine, and you have an excellent appetiser that is Swiss to gastronomic gratification.

The active ingredient to any Swiss speciality, I must point out, is the fact that it was due to Swiss participation, or at least intervention, that the dish evolved.

Take, for example, *Nytlä* – rice cooked in cream from the Uri Alps. It could have been Germanic, French or Italian in essence, but it was owing to the harsh alpine climate that the herdsmen of Uri specially concocted this dish. The mixture of rice, cream, salt, milk and butter not only provided the men with something solid and tasty, *Nytlä* has also gone down in culinary history as a recipe that proves to be just as welcome in winter in the foothills today.

Who would have guessed the great Auguste Escoffier together with Swiss hotelier Cesar Ritz began whipping soufflés at the Hotel National in Lucerne? Or that inventor-chocolatier Daniel Peter was the first to actually hold a solidified bar of milk chocolate back in 1875? We are not often reminded that the electric oven we now overlook as just another appliance was invented by the Bernina Hotel in 1889. There is no resting on their laurels, they push on ... towards being inducted successfully into globally accepted and respected diets with Dr. Bircher-Benner's müesli breakfast and arguably the best way to fry potatoes.

Foreign Influence

Despite the fact that the Swiss enjoy a traditional meal of meat and potatoes, the growing trend of sampling foreign cooking has taken city dwellers by storm. Japanese *sushi* and *teppanyaki*, an endless menu of Asian delicacies from Chinese and Vietnamese restaurants, and spicy hot Thai and Mexican dishes are leaving singe marks on wandering palates.

It makes perfect sense that tourists are the ones who dictate which restaurants make it and which don't.

If you have just arrived in Switzerland without any culinary experience to save your life, don't panic. In due course, you will want to prolong your time in the kitchen, finding out what makes their *Basler Mehlsuppe* so brown or their *Emmentaler* mutton stew so heartily wholesome. Who knows, you may even end up perfecting cooking skills every weekend and inviting friends over to try out some veritable homecooked meal.

WHEN YOU INVITE ...

The Swiss, being a courteous lot, will be too polite to tell you pig's brain or pan-fried crocodile burgers aren't their cup of tea. If you are going out of your way to soup up an exotic evening of tastebud twisters, it's all right to run the menu by them before donning the apron at five in the morning.

WHEN YOU ARE INVITED ...

When you are invited to a meal, go with something in hand: a bottle of wine or a box of after-dinner sweets will help the meal go down a lot smoother, not to mention allowing your gracious host or hostess to feel appreciated for the time spent slaving in the kitchen. This is a European practice hardly confined to the Swiss.

BREADS

A lot of this breakfast carbohydrate is consumed over the three main meals of the day and I can't say I blame them. A friend of ours lived in an apartment directly over a baker's for a torturous year and a half. Freshly baked breads do weird things to one's olfactory at 4:30 am ...

The Swiss like their bread crusty and full of fibre. I spent three months scouring local bakers for a more tender white bread and came up with nothing. Their softer breads resemble braided tresses and are delicious with the jams they preserve religiously every July and August. Croissants and baguettes are acceptably French-influenced but nobody's complaining about the Swiss version. You can purchase them fresh at the baker's or in the supermarkets where they are mass-produced but nevertheless *aussi frais*.

Two specialities in the bread line is fruit bread a la Glarus (*Glarner Früchtebrot*) in the Swiss-German parts and Panattoni in the Swiss-Italian regions.

CHEESES

Dairy farmers since the time the early Romans lorded over Helvetian herdsmen, the Swiss have made the art of cheesemaking more than a vocation. Indeed cheese manufacturing calls for exacting requirements, for example inspecting and passing as genuinely Swiss the size of holes in every Appenzeller cheese wheel!

A single Emmental cheese weighing 120 kg requires approximately 1,500 litres of fresh milk for its production. That's a very big amount of milk for a relatively small loaf of cheese. Yet Emmental cheese sells like hot cakes at annual cheese harvests.

Other cheeses you will meet include Sbrinz, Gruyère, and Appenzeller – three that have made Swiss cheese the preferred choice.

Famous cheese dishes include fondue (Emmental and Gruyère cheese melted in a communal caquelon), *Ramequin* (cheese pie), *Gratin Montagnard* (cheese soufflé), *Kartoffelgratin* (potatoes au gratin), *Kartoffel-Käse-Auflauf* (potato and cheese casserole) and *Käserösti* (cheese *rösti*).

WINES AND SPIRITS

Total teetotallers are uncommon in Switzerland. Friends studying hotel catering in Cesar Ritz confirmed that Swiss wines produced in the western region, from the Chablis vineyards (Sion) to Bonvillars (Neuchâtel), are not only worth the Sfr. 10–15 one pays for them, they are delicious accompaniments to many dishes of the local seasonal fare.

During the last ripening week of September and the first harvesting week of October, Chasselas (or Gutedel), Sylvaners, Gamay, Merlot, and Pinot Noir grapes are gathered precariously from steep embankments and slopes.

In the Valais region down south where the sunshine is warmer, Fendant and Dôle are the bacchantic favourites. Young white wines delicious because of their fruitiness and clarity include Arquebuse, Grandson Chasselas and Les Nonnes. Reds like the Pinot-Gamay and the Hallebarde Salvagnin are extremely potable with red meats.

Fruit brandies like Willamine and Träsch are evergreen after-dinner spirits. *Kaffee fertig* (Swiss brandy in a hot, sweet coffee) has a delicate taste and aroma.

MEATS

Step into the neighbourhood butcher's and your nose will be accosted by the smell of freshly butchered cattle, its scrag end sometimes still hanging from the gambrel. This is the place to purchase beef, mutton, veal, pork, chicken, rabbit, horsemeat, sausages, salami, razor-thin Mesolcino or Prosciutto, bacon, cured hams, meatloafs, terrines, patés, and even internal organs such as liver, kidneys and intestines.

The Swiss prefer a hot soup, a simple sandwich or cold cuts with sausages for lunch, leaving a little more room at dinner for meat dishes. Not unheard of is the eccentric dish from Geneva called *Pommes farcies* (stuffed apples) which I thought to be a convenient meal – dinner and dessert in one dish. *Pot-au-feu* (literally 'pot on the fire') and *Borsch* (a healthy beef soup with chunks of fresh vegetables) are common in Swiss households. Every canton appears to have some outlandish speciality handed down from creative grandmothers since days of yore. Don't be surprised if they pick their own vegetables from a small plot of land in their backyard. When they want fresh, they do mean fresh!

Some unmistakable ne'er-go-awry meat dishes to survive this century of insipid fast-foodies must include *Zürcher Geschnetzeltes* (Zurich veal), *Süübäggli und suure Gummeli* (in Swiss-German dialect: pork rump with sour potatoes) and *Papet à la Vaud* (three types of Vaudoise sausages in a pot of simmering leeks, potatoes, onions and wine).

FRUIT AND VEGETABLES

At the farmers' market, I found purchasing fresh fruit and vegetables a bargainable option to the supermarkets. The Swiss are very picky with the freshness of the produce and it would be unthinkable that someone's chicory or *poivron rouge* is anything other than in perfect shape and colour. The farmers' market is normally set up once or twice a week and are chemical-free homegrown produce.

What you find in the Migros or Coop won't be too shabby either. It seems only the cream of the crops end up in Swiss-bound cartons, train or truck-sped to supermarkets everywhere. Not amazingly, it was Migros, the largest supermarket chain, which revolutionised transportation, smoothing distribution channels and paving the way for other marketing moguls to follow suit.

POTATOES

The English have chips, Americans have baked potatoes, but the Swiss have made this simple 17th century import an ubiquitous companion to practically any meal. Potatoes can be baked as in the case of *Birre und stock*, stewed as in the Central Swiss Bean Pot, gratined as in the *Fribourgoise Kartoffelgratin* or fried to a golden hue as in *rösti*. They can even be artlessly boiled to dip in a *Stupfete* (herb fondue without cheese).

When you trolley down the aisle looking for these little *pommes de terre*, you can take in a mini-lecture on a poster nearby. There are many different kinds of tubers which react to different ways of heating. If you're not a potato fan, at least you won't end up hating them either.

FISH

Perch, trout, the *Zugsee Rötel*, dace, pike and the *l'omble chevalier* are some of the inland water creatures that have found their way to Swiss supermarkets.

If you don't like fishy smells and aren't used to freshwater fish, be prepared to strew a handful of herbs on them prior to cooking. Some are oven-baked and some wrapped in waxy paper (*papillote*) drowned in dry white wine, but rarely are they ever steamed.

DESSERTS

We have come to the core of the mystery at last; what Friedrich Schiller's William Tell did to the apple he spliced. A foray into Swiss cookbooks will reveal many ingenious methods of preparing this species of *Malus Sylvestris*. The flavourful *Apfel Bröisi* (fried apples with stale French rolls) takes recycling out of the landfills into the kitchen.

Summertime yields the greatest amount of fruits. Wild berries of every ilk get trodden on, plucked, peckered, pressed, pinched and preserved. Bread cakes such as the Basler version of *Kirschenbrottorte*

121

(cherry-bread cake) and *Zwetschgenauflauf* (plum casserole) are intelligent if not ecological solutions in dealing with surplus.

One of the most tempting cakes I've had the privilege to savour is the *Rüeblitorte* (carrot cake). Carrot cake is not exceptional to this country – you can find it on dessert trays the world over. I persist in believing, however, that the Swiss carrot cake is the best owing to the shot of *Kirschwasser* (cherry brandy) neatly slipped in between whipping the eggs and adding the lemon peel.

A South African friend, famous in our circle for reproducing the most delicious cakes and desserts without ever glancing up from her kneading block, has the most marvellous gift of discerning ingredients in desserts merely by tasting them. When this doyenne of desserts tried some *Basler Leckerli*, she was stumped by the lack of ginger in these squarish sweet biscuits. After some research on its history, it turned out the Basler bakers did use ginger in their biscuits six hundred years ago. Today, candied and lemon peels are substituted for the spicy root to make this dessert, which my friend still claims to be less than the best. Not one to quibble with her, this soft biscuit is still our favourite when it comes to finding something to dunk in a cup of espresso or *café au lait*.

Swiss dishes are truly instinctive when it comes to economising, recycling or cooking leftovers in the quickest and most sumptuous way. Here are a few recipes that promise not to break your back.

Fried Apples (Apfel Bröisi)

500 g (1 lb) stale French rolls or bread
1 kg (2 lbs) tart apples
4 tablespoons butter
4 tablespoons sugar
6 tablespoons fresh butter
a dash of cinnamon powder

Slice the bread and apples as thinly as possible. Heat the butter in a skillet adding bread and sugar to mix until crisp. Add the apple slices and turn them constantly to ensure even cooking. Add the fresh butter and let it melt. Sprinkle with some cinnamon powder and serve on warm dishes immediately.

Central Swiss Bean Pot (Innerschweizer Bohnentopf)

250 g (8 oz) mutton
250 g (8 oz) smoked neck of pork
cooking oil
1 kg (2 lbs) string beans, cut into bite-size lengths
250 g (8 oz) carrots, thinly sliced
salt
1 kg (2 lbs) new potatoes (the smaller the better), peeled

Cut mutton and pork into small pieces. Heat the oil and brown the meats, adding the beans and the thinly sliced carrots. Add salt to taste and enough hot water to cook the vegetables through. Cover the vegetables with peeled and lightly salted potatoes and simmer well for an hour. Serve with rustic *paysan* bread and a light red wine.

Zurich Veal (Zürcher Geschnetzeltes)

500 g (1 lb) veal cutlet
flour
4 tablespoons butter
2 small onions, chopped
$^1/_2$ cup white wine
salt and pepper
$^1/_2$ cup cream

Slice veal into narrow strips and dust with flour. Heat butter in a skillet and sauté the chopped onions until they are tender. Brown the meat over high heat and add white wine, salt and pepper and cook for another minute or two. Thicken with the cream and serve with either *rösti* (recipe on p. 126) or fragrant rice.

Beef Soup (Pot-au-feu)

12 cups of water
1 tablespoon salt
1 savoy cabbage (cut into strips)
1 stem of leek
500 g (1 lb) carrots
1 celery root, quartered
600 g (1$^1/_4$ lbs) potatoes, cubed
1 small swede (rutabaga), cubed (optional)
1 large onion
2 cloves garlic
1 kg (2 lbs) marbled beef
2 soup bones
4 whole peppercorns
1 bay leaf

Bring salted water to a boil with the vegetables, onion and garlic. Add meat, bones, peppercorns and bay leaf. Simmer on low heat for 2 hours or until meat is tender. Serve with horseradish sauce, mustard and cranberries or eat it with buttered rye bread.

Fondue Neuchâtel

1 clove garlic (more if preferred)
2 cups dry white wine
4 teaspoons lemon juice
$2^1/_2$ to $3^1/_2$ cups grated Emmentaler
$2^1/_2$ to $3^1/_2$ cups grated Gruyère
1 shot glass of cherry brandy (*Kirschwasser*)
1 heaped tablespoon cornstarch
dash of pepper, nutmeg and paprika
French bread (cubed) – about 200 g (7 oz) per person

Rub the caquelon with the garlic, and heat the white wine and lemon juice in it. Gradually add cheese and continue to stir under medium to high heat. Mix the cherry brandy with the cornstarch and add to caquelon. Season with pepper, paprika and nutmeg. Remove from the gas stove (this won't work on an electric stove), place over an alcohol burner and begin the meal. Bread cubes are dipped into the cheesy mixture. Serve hot tea or chilled white wine, but never water.

Having fondue in the privacy of someone's home is one of the most sociable ways of getting to know each other better.

Rösti

1 kg (2 lbs) potatoes boiled in their skin
1 tablespoon salt
3–4 tablespoons shortening or cooking oil

Peel and mash boiled potatoes and sprinkle salt over them. Heat the shortening in a skillet and add potatoes to brown for 20–30 minutes over low heat. Turn to check if the mashed potato is browning nicely. Cover with a plate and turn the potato pancake over. Return to the skillet to brown the other side. Serve with a green salad and large glasses of iced lemon tea.

Carrot Cake (Rüeblitorte)

6 eggs (separated)
1^1/$_2$ cups sugar
grated peel of 1 lemon
1 shot glass of *Kirschwasser*
3 cups grated almonds
250 g (8 oz) grated raw carrot
3 tablespoons flour
icing sugar

Beat egg yolks with sugar until fluffy. Add lemon peel and *Kirschwasser*. Whip egg whites until stiff and fold in almonds, carrot and flour before adding to egg yolk mixture. Turn into greased and floured round pan and bake at medium heat (180°C/350°F) for an hour or until lightly browned. Cool for half an hour before dusting the surface with icing sugar.

There are many cookbooks found in Payot libraries all over the country. Betty Bossi is a fictitious name whose recipe booklets can be found in almost any Swiss-Romande kitchen cabinet. And when all else fails, having Swiss breads and mountain-fresh water every day doesn't sound so bad.

Chapter Ten

ALL ABOUT BUSINESS

The first commandment for Swiss building firms is "We never lose sight of feasibility." It might as well be the maxim for all the other economic sectors because Switzerland has no natural resources, no raw materials, little fertile land – and yet it is one of the wealthiest industrialised countries in the world. The feasibility of such an achievement is not hard to imagine as the tradition of hard work and responsibility in the Swiss workplace is legendary. A business major who graduated from the European University in Fontanivent once remarked that Switzerland's self-made success story was largely due to the efficiency of its people. Efficiency is self-sufficiency, and it is true that the entire country appears to be obsessed with running employees and businesses like well-oiled cogs in a wheel.

Arriving in Switzerland in the early 1990s was tantamount to having 'made it' for the husband and me, not that making it was effortless or had cost nothing.

Foreign investments and trade with the European unionised countries were skyrocketing and the strong Swiss franc had allowed even piddling foreigners like us to reap the benefits of high bank interest rates: an eye-boggling $5^1/2\%$ for a savings bank account, when fixed deposits in some countries didn't realise beyond 3%! Taxes soared right along with it and so, prior to the devastating recession of 1993, all was as right as rain. Every business contact, opportunity and venture was accepted as congenially as the fall of communism in the former Soviet Union.

The broad-range diversity of the Swiss economy, with internationally competitive firms in the banking, insurance, machinery, chemical, pharmaceutical and trading industries, created a fruitful environment for new growth and avenues to further improve international business relations.

It is no state secret that Switzerland is highly dependent on foreign trade. Exports make an important contribution to Switzerland's prosperity. Swiss watchmakers sell over 90% of their output on foreign markets. The chemical industry exports about 85%, textiles and clothing manufacturers over 70% and the food sector about 65%. Swiss insurers earn 63% of their revenue abroad and the banking industry 33%.

In more recent years, the exchange of Research and Development information, notably with Japan, has increased the visibility of Switzerland's own involvement in integrating smaller research institutions. Establishing the Swiss Centre for Electronics and Microtechnology (CSEM) contributed substantially to boosting economic growth during the otherwise slow-recovery post-recession period.

The 1995 Swiss economic outlook has been forecast to show more investment-driven growth in exporting construction equipment. According to a study by the Swiss Federal Institute of Technology's Centre for the Research of Economic Activity, Switzerland's private sector investment is returning to healthy growth. For a country as small as Switzerland, optimism has an important place for the feasibility of its continued expansion.

THE CHALLENGE TODAY

The challenge today is still fighting the evils brought about by unemployment and the general listlessness that pervades whenever governmental benefits counteract the incentive to seek alternative employment. The Swiss are not inherently lazy, but the trend seems to be a disinterest in further training when the chips are down and retrenchment is severe. Public places such as parks and cinemas appear to be full of people capable of working, but friends we spoke to said that some of these unemployed were uncertain if their expertise had expired or their speciality in a specific field made redundant.

The three main causes of structural unemployment are the lack of incentive, a discrepancy between skills required and skills offered, and institutional inflexibility. The buck actually stops at the government to create a framework that supports radical career adjustments and changes while increasing the incentive to get back on the payroll. The government is thus to subordinate itself to the role of a surrogate mother, reestablishing a healthier relationship between wages and an acceptable standard of living.

Distribution of the working population (survey done in 1997)

Primary sector:	4.62% or 176,000
Secondary sector:	26.8% or 1,018,000
Tertiary sector:	68.6% or 2,609,000
Total working population:	3,803,000
Share of foreigners:	936,000

WAGES

The Swiss wage policy is as inflexible as an arthritic with rheumatism thrown in for good measure. It ensures that rehabilitation is all but impossible.

The allocative function of wages is compromised by the government's redistributive aims. The simple economic rule, unapplied in Switzerland, states that changes in pay have to be in accord with changes in production. When production suffers, workers' wages should take a setback as well. However, since the last recession in 1945, Switzerland has had escalating high salaries and welcome unemployment benefits.

State provision, when productivity is high, is great for the country, but during less favourable times, many an economist started begging the government to revise labour policies.

Salaries vary a fair bit between regions and kinds of industries. The service sector pays better than manufacturing as does the private over the state sectors. If you were to work for the state, for example as a postman or an administrative clerk, chances are you will be paid according to your job classification and age. On the other hand, if you worked as a secretary in the private sector, job performance and productivity will be the deciding factors for the amount of your take-home cheque. One of the best incentives young gungho preppies have to enter the private sector is the additional 14th month bonus offered at the end of the year.

Women in Switzerland in general earn around 33% less than their male counterparts, the reason being society's prejudiced view over the so-called traditionally 'female' jobs, such as teaching in lower levels and sales. With the rapidly rising cost of living in the cities, women are opting to work even for lower incomes to help pay the household bills. The survey on spending between 1950 and 1990 revealed that the bulk of income went towards education, transportation, insurance and taxes. Clothing, food and personal effects cannot rival the proportion spent on the 'more important' commodities.

The Swiss are reticent to begin with and to ask about their salaries is in bad taste, or downright rude. A few of them, however, don't think twice about revealing how much they earn. Nurses coming straight out of the examination hall with a certificate of completion can look forward to about Sfr. 4,000 per month. This is not the rule of thumb, as their salary also depends upon which hospital employs them, and what their duties entail. A secretary earns between Sfr. 3,500 and Sfr. 4,000, and a secondary school teacher may earn a relatively high salary of Sfr. 5,000 and above.

Wages have had their peaks and troughs. It is hard to determine pay and pay increments, though across the board they are comparatively high in above-average brackets but low for those who work in factories or those paid by the hour.

THE BREADWINNER

Traditionally, earning the household bread was the man's role but more and more women executives are hanging up the apron to slip into something more powerful. Single-parent breadwinners are now a dying breed in bigger cities. Grandparents are babysitting their grandchildren as both parents give their waking hours to earning more money so that they can afford more children.

Quite ironic, really.

WORKING HOURS

Hardworking. Conscientious. Reliable. Punctual. Efficient. It isn't amazing that these accolades all point to any Swiss who's *got* a job in Switzerland. To begin with, the Swiss cultivate good habits. They start early in order to finish on time. With an average of 43 hours a week depending on the nature of the work, one need not raise an eyebrow when companies start shelling out big bonuses by end December. They are certainly not in the business of tardiness. The amazing thing is, this isn't just corporate policy; it appears the entire country works this way!

131

Depending on which canton you work in, working hours vary but slightly. In general, Monday through Friday, the hours are 8 am to 5 pm with one or two hours' break at midday. Saturdays do not normally constitute a working day, but there are exceptions.

INSURANCE

The State Pension Fund

AHV, or the Old-age and Survivor's Insurance, is a social programme launched in 1947. The purpose of AHV is to cover pensioners' basic needs. Men generally retire at age 65, and women at 62. The AHV is funded by both the employer and the employee. Each pays 5.05% of the employee's wage. The AHV is income-based, which means the more you earn, the more you contribute. The pension amounts to a minimum of Sfr. 900 and a maximum of Sfr. 1,800 per month. Even the maximum amount is insufficient to cover basic living expenses. Company pension and personal savings are the other two insurance plans for retirees.

A married woman is not subjected to a separate pension, but benefits only from her husband's. When her husband passes on, she receives a widow's pension that is smaller than the regular benefit.

Company Pension Plans

Since 1972, the introduction of the Company Pension Plan was the first step to assuring a continued standard of living after retirement. Similar to the AHV, both employer and employee are expected to contribute 9–10% of the employee's income.

Personal Savings

The last and the least feasible for low-income employees, personal savings are especially indispensable when one grows older and medical bills start piling up. Numerous insurance schemes now offer tax privileges but, by and large, personal savings in Switzerland don't help much unless they amount to at least Sfr. 50,000.

HAVE BUSINESS WILL TRAVEL

Switzerland should be looked at as a cluster of small but dynamic regional companies. It is fairly common to travel by plane from Geneva's Cointrin to Zurich's Kloten airport regularly or by train to different regions of the country. The busy network of company branches and franchises has been known to bring even the most office-bound executive outside for a day of running about.

There are several flights each day between Zurich, Geneva and Basel. Most prefer to travel by train as journeys rarely exceed 3 hours.

NATIONAL FAIRS

Switzerland is very cosmopolitan and therefore ideal for conventions and conferences. Three official national fairs are the Swiss Industries Fair in Basel in April, the Comptoir Suisse National Fair in Lausanne in September, and the OLMA (Swiss Agriculture and Dairy Farming Fair) in St. Gallen in October.

POWER LUNCHES AND DRESS CODE

Over *shabu-shabu*, while picking over *kimchee* in a Korean restaurant, power lunches have caught on in many large cities. Advertising executives in Hugo Boss jackets careening round narrow Geneva streets in their flashy Mercedes convertibles are the motivative springboard for many university freshmen.

Europe is the fashion continent of the world and this is not exclusive to the Italians or French. The Swiss are nattily dressed and easily recognised by the brand of their suit or dress. Most will settle for something prêt-à-porter and smart and avoid flamboyant colours with fanciful tailoring. Excellent places to purchase reasonably-priced clothes are at Hennes & Mauritz, Globus, PKZ and C & A.

WORK ETHICS

The Swiss pride themselves in honouring their contracts, keeping the hours required at the office and doing their job with utmost efficiency and a deep sense of responsibility. Of all the Swiss companies I made contact with, everyone kept their rendezvous and appointments as promised to me verbally over the telephone. Their integrity is almost as formidable as their dedication to national productivity.

Many foreigners come to Switzerland for short spells – to learn the ropes of a trade, to hold seminars or on attachment to parent companies for special projects. Those who come have remarked on the cleanliness, not merely on the exterior, but in the way the Swiss conduct business. One of the most memorable interviews I had was with an employment company who gave 110% in trying to help me secure a job situation at a graduate school in Lausanne.

The standards of Swiss companies are high, with performance and loyalty enviously guarded. No doubt there are black sheep who denigrate the polished reputation of those incorruptibles. Backstabbing is not unheard of, company politicking occurring wherever ambition lurks, but it is fair to say that most stick to the rules when playing climb-the-executive-ladder games.

manager if a problem arises or there are differences of opinion. Misunderstanding or miscommunication is quite often the reason two persons cannot get along and it only aggravates a bad situation when one shuns the person in question.

THE COMMERCIAL LANGUAGE OF BUSINESS

There are already three languages used in Switzerland. If you are monolingual, then you are way behind. When I attended night classes in French, I had classmates from Buenos Aires and Johannesburg who were interior designers. It is a common practice to send executives to improve, polish or learn the language of the region.

Business is conducted in French, German or Italian, but the trend towards integrating English is being reinforced in large companies.

WHO'S WHO IN THE INNOVATIVE LINE

Gerd Binnig and Heinrich Rohrer: Invented the microscope for scanning tunnelling and atomic force in 1982. Rohrer received the Nobel Prize for Physics in 1986.

George Louis Lesage: Invented the electric telegraph in 1774.

Carl Gustav Jung (1875–1961): Psychologist, developed analytical psychology.

Rolex, Switzerland: Invented the first waterproof watch in 1927.

Louis Favre (1826–1879): Key engineer who constructed the St. Gotthard tunnel.

Othmar Ammann (1879–1965): Engineer who was credited with building the George Washington Bridge, New York.

Paul Scherrer (1890–1969): Chemist and physicist; researched the structure of crystals with X-rays.

Paul Herman Müller (1899–1965): Chemist and inventor of DDT. 1948 Nobel Prize winner in Medicine.

Julius Maggi (1846–1912): Industrialist who developed food concentrates and convenience foods.

135

Carl Elsener: Inventor of the Swiss knife in 1884. Patented three years later in 1897.

Le Corbusier (Charles-Edourd Jeanneret) 1887–1965: Painter and architect; founder of modern architecture.

THE TWELVE I'S FOR SUCCESS

This is a summary from an article delivered by Hans-Ulrich Doerig, Vice-Chairman of the Board of Directors of Credit Suisse at the ISC symposium in St. Gallen on 31 May 1994.

The twelve I's are skewed towards those Macbethian few who want more from a job than basic job satisfaction.

The First I: Integrity

Personal integrity including fairness, loyalty and team spirit will always be the most important requirements if you intend to succeed as the manager of tomorrow.

The Second I: Interrogative-integral Attitude

In short, it is the desire to learn, to acquire analytical skills and to have a systematic approach and openness to think through different scenarios in difficult situations. It is vital that the manager is able to communicate his or her own vision while cultivating 'intellectual inquisitiveness'.

The Third I: International-intercultural Skills

For Swiss managers, a command of three languages is a basic requirement. Families have to welcome work-related relocations, even though that will increase the potential for conflict in situations where both marriage partners have a career.

The Fourth I: Intensive-identifying approach

Managers should identify with the work they do and see it as a vocation. The attitude should be positive and a sustainable basis created for the qualities required – stamina, discipline, initiative, enthusiasm and resilience to stress. Without this sense of identification, work will always remain a chore and never become a source of pleasure.

The Fifth I: Innovation
Innovation is possible only when people are ready to weigh up risks with an open mind. In short, risk acceptance and risk limitation are vital to an innovative corporate culture.

The Sixth I: Immunity
The managers of the future need to take a relaxed view of constant change, adaptation and reorientation. They should not perceive change as a threat in the long term.

The Seventh I: Integrating intermediary
Ludwig Erhard said: "Compromise is the art of dividing the cake so skilfully that everyone believes they have the largest slice." The successful manager operates as a leader, team member and stabiliser. He or she is the one who will motivate all other members to work towards achieving the common goal.

The Eighth I: Intrapreneurship
What is particularly required in younger managers is the ability to implement – in other words, doing it right. Results-oriented management is more important than the verbal articulation of a vision.

The Ninth I: Improvisation
Without flexibility and a capacity for improvisation, failure is inevitable. Managers must be able to act as 'empowerer', or 'soft coach', even troubleshooter or pacifier.

The Tenth I: Intuition
Decision-making without intuition is dead off centre.

The Eleventh I: Intercommunicating-instructing Skills
Given the rapid pace of change, managers' responsibility as instructors of their staff is increased.

The Twelfth I: Introspective
To understand their environment and manage their staff, managers need to understand and manage themselves. Asking themselves the questions "Who am I and what do I want?" or "Am I prepared to take unpopular decisions as well?" may be more revealing than they think.

— Chapter Eleven —

LAST RESORTS AND
LAST REMARKS

Sniff... Sniff... Sniff...

Our last month in Switzerland was sentimental to say the least, and traumatic to boot. Pregnant 20 weeks with our son Myron, the weepy emotions that welled up in me can only be produced by hormones and a mixture of premature grief at the loss of friends.

Parting is more than 'such sweet sorrow'; it is bitter, nasty and downright bilious. Calling up freight forwarders, arranging to pick up empty cartons, clearing debts and collecting deposits are time- and energy-consuming. To clear out of our apartment, we had to enlist the help of tried and trusted friends to clean, scrub, uncalque and polish the furnishings for the final *état-des-lieux*. Special thanks go out to

A memorable afternoon's packing during happier moments before the reality of leaving Switzerland actually hit us.

Dominique (the one-person army) who spent three of her lunch hours on her knees and on her toes doing the dirty job few would endeavour to accomplish.

Switzerland had been to both Moses and me a learning experience, dealing with a culture that is as varied as its cheeses. The intense privacy allowed each individual had been the most tell-taling trait of the Swiss people. Respect and responsible parenting are two treasures we have accepted as parting gifts. This is not to say we have had a trouble-free life there, but rather the no-nonsense approach to living has proven its precious point. Admittedly the Swiss are law-abiding people. They are also a very hardworking, hard-playing sort who prefer a neutral existence to fisticuffing with their neighbours. I applaud their efforts to continue in this vein.

Selling our furniture, car, and 'rubbish', as the husband calls our third-hand goods, was tiring and endless. This is something expatriates cannot look forward to but must if they want to recoup on some losses.

What is it that makes Switzerland such a hospitable country? I believe it is what makes any place home – chiefly friends who treat you like family. There have been so many occasions to celebrate the gift of friendship, such as the ones we had found at the Art Centre, in church, and in the surrounding schools. As we rummaged our belongings to find remnants of our stay in Switzerland, scores of photographs spilled out on the living room floor. It could have been a lump in my throat which betrayed my uneasiness, or the baby giving me heartburn. In any case, nothing could have made leaving easier.

It makes me think of the early days as we tried to settle into this physically frigid country whose kindness came from sympathetic Swiss who wanted to help but couldn't communicate in our language. For those whose experience was not as pleasant, and for newcomers, here is a list of some helpful numbers and addresses. The idea is to know that there can be answers to nagging questions you have brewing in the back of your mind.

Realising there can be help made a great difference to the way we settled in in the country we will always know as our first home.

Police: 117

Fire brigade: 118

Ambulance: 144 (in most cantons)

Swiss rail information: 040/67.10.50

Weather forecast: 162

State of the roads: 163

Crisis line: 143

Fault reporting: 175

Time: 161

Subscribers' numbers within Switzerland, nearest chemist, doctor, dentist, national enquiries: 111

Motoring assistance: 140

Calls abroad not dialled direct: 1159

Anglophone SA
15, quai du Cheval Blanc
1227 Carouge/Switzerland
e-mail: anglofon@iprolink.com
Internet: http://www.anglolake.com

Touring Club of Switzerland (Touring Club der Schweiz)
9, rue Pierro-Fatio
1211 Geneva 3
Tel: 022/ 737.12.12
Tel: (24-hour breakdown service) 022.358.00

Swiss Automotive Club (Automobil-Club der Schweiz)
Wasserwerkgasse 39
3011 Bern
Tel: 031/328.31.11
Fax: 031/311.03.10

Swiss Camping Association (Verband Schweizer Campings)
Seestrasse 119, 3800
Interlaken
Tel: 036/23.35.23

Budget Rent-a-car
Geneva Airport: 022/798.22.53 (Arrival Hall)
Lugano Airport: 091/611.10.48 (Arrival Hall)
Zurich Airport: 01/813.31.31 (Parkhaus B)

Swiss SA
Hauptsitz Viktoriastr. 21
3050 Bern
Tel: 031/342.11.11
Fax: 031/342.25.49

American Express International Inc., Geschäftsreisen
Seefeldstr, 214, 8008, Zurich
Tel: 01/384.64.06

Swiss Bank Corporation
Basel: 061/288.20.20
Geneva: 022/375.75.75
Zurich: 01/223.11.11

Credit Suisse Head Office
Verwaltung Postfach 8070
Zurich
Fax: 01/332.55.55

Swiss Youth Hostel Association (open to all ages)
(Auberges de jeunesse suisses/ Schweizerischer Bund für Jugendher-
bergen/Alloggi svizzeri per giovani)
Mutschellenstrasse 116
Postfach 8038 Zurich
Tel: 01/482.45.61
Fax: 01/482 45.78

or in the **Suisse-Romand area:**
Leopold-Robert 65
2300 La Chaux-de-Fonds
Tel: 039/23.78.51
Fax: 039/23.78.52

The Switzerland Advisor (travel services)
P.O. Box 103, 1000, Lausanne 19
Fax: 021/784.41.14

Montreux Jazz Festival Reservations/Information
Tel: 021/ 31.34567

Swiss National Tourist Office
Gare de Bern
Case Postale 2700
3001 Bern
Tel: 031/22.76.76

Red Cross
Ave. de la Gare 10
1003 Lausanne
Tel: 021/329.00.29

ENGLISH-SPEAKING GROUPS

Focus International Career Services
(Non-profit career resource centre for professionals)
17, Route de Collex
1293 Bellevue Geneva
Tel: 022/774.16.39

British and American Club
Av. de l'Avant-Poste 4
1005, Lausanne
Contact: Mrs Birrer
Tel: 021/323.40.44

International Club of Lausanne
Av. de Valmont 14
1010 Lausanne
Tel: 021/653.23.88

American Resource Centre (Basel)
Tel/Fax: 061.28.15
e-mail: arc@iprolink.ch

International Club of Berne
Tel: 031/941.36.49
Fax: 031/922.02.62

American Women's Club of Geneva
Tel: 022/736.01.20
Fax: 022/735.03.32

Singapore Club (Geneva)
Tel: 022/752.46.35

Asian Ladies Group of Zurich
Tel/Fax: 01.822.29.58

Australian-Swiss Chamber of Commerce (Zurich)
Tel: 01.262.11.12

Canadian-Swiss Association (Zurich)
Tel: 01.721.12.80

Fax: 01. 721.12.90

English-Speaking Club of Zurich
Tel: 01. 831. 29.49

Professional Women's Group(Zurich)
Tel; 01. 262.82.94

USEFUL INTERNET ADDRESSES/WEBSITES:

www.ziwa.com/ (Zurich International Women's Association ZIWA)

www.easyJet.com (Great airfares)

www.sbb.ch (Swiss Federal Railroads schedule)

www.schweizferien.ch (Information about Swiss cities, current snow conditions, special offers)

www.ethz.ch/swiss/Switzerland_Info.html (General info)

www.tte.ch/Switzerland/index.html (Tourismus Team Europe)

heiwww.unige.ch/switzerland/ (Useful search engine)

www.switzerland.isyours.com/ (Swiss accounts/working/immigration/starting a business)

www.switzerland.com/ (Travel/business/interest rates/society/news)

www.tele.ch/ (Television related, in German)

www.swissinfo.org/eng/ (Highly informative)

E-mail:info@switzerland.isyours.com

CULTURAL QUIZ

SCENARIO 1

You have overcome the transitional culture shock after befriending many Swiss friends in the office. Besides wanting to enliven the home somewhat, you plan your Friday soirée with great panache and decide to cook something from your home country (for example, ostrich meat in red wine). Do you:

A Plan everything in secret and announce everyone is invited during Friday afternoon tea-break?

B Issue posh invitations to everyone a week earlier?

C Personally go around to those you want to invite about a week earlier and tell them the menu you will be preparing?

D Call them the night before to encourage them to turn up?

Answer

C. This is not to say the other answers are wrong or they shouldn't be done. The Swiss like to plan their activities ahead especially if it concerns the weekend. Having to find a babysitter requires time as well, and it's a safer bet to pass round the menu for feedback before the dishes actually go a-circulating.

SCENARIO 2

For the third night in a row, your neighbours have been keeping you awake until 2 am because the World Cup Semifinals and Finals are being televised live on Eurosport. Do you:

A Ignore them during the night but terrorise them by leaving threatening notes in their letter-boxes the next morning?

B Assert yourself by calling them Sh*theads via an open window?

C Call the police?

D Try to reason with them face-to-face first, but that failing, buy earplugs?

Answer

D is the most effective answer simply because the World Cup Finals is a national craze. It would be pointless to call the police in this particular case because it is an epidemic nuisance and it is impossible to quell the roar until all is over. Terrorising them or calling them names might get you into trouble if they happen to be vindictive. The best solution is to cope with it any way you can.

SCENARIO 3

Sitting by the lake feeding the swans, you find yourself the unlikely target of some unsavoury character oozing oily charm and *dragueur* looks. Do you:

A Stare back indignantly and walk off with your head held high?

B Ignore the person but walk off quickly towards a crowded street?

C Turn away with a look of contempt and keep feeding the swans?

D Confront him and tell him to shove off?

Answer

B. Ignoring unwanted attention is the most effective way of dealing with people who find staring at others pleasurable. Since this situation cannot be properly explained or guaranteed to be harmless, it is wisest to move out of a secluded area to a place where some help, if needed, is quickly found. If you live in a slightly more remote town and are obviously non-European looking, you will get a lot of attention from the locals. Many of them don't mean much harm by looking, so don't get too defensive if your spouse is being given the perfunctory gazing.

SCENARIO 4

You have just arrived in Switzerland. When you are thinking of insurance policies, do you:

A Purchase one for the car?
B Purchase one for the house?
C Purchase one for your health? or
D Purchase one for all three?

Answer

D. This is not so much a choice as it is a prerequisite. Switzerland is known for playing safe and insuring the gross can be more an advantage in the long term. This does not mean you'll be a pauper at the end of the year as you will have a range of insurance policies to choose from. Because you are obliged to purchase all of the above, don't try to escape or ignore the commune's repeated efforts to insure you, your family and your assets.

SCENARIO 5

In the rush to attend the year-end conference in Sonloup near les Avants you discover to your horror that you haven't any small change to buy the ticket from the automatic machine. Do you:

A Hop onto the *funiculaire* anyway and pray that the ticket officer is on tea break.

B Ask anyone for change so that you can buy the ticket with a clean conscience.

C Feign ignorance of the language when the leather-clad officer starts grilling you with embarrassing questions.

D Get on the *funiculaire* but explain the situation and show him you have money but no small change.

Answer

B is the best thing to do, and unless it's after eleven and there's not a soul in sight do you attempt *D*. *A* is frequently done but is not advisable as is answer *C* because the ticket officer does a lot of spot checks and is humourless when it comes to the language barrier.

SCENARIO 6

Of all the concierges in the world, you had to be under the same roof as Madame Slowpoke who is 76 years old and who has the memory of a 90-year-old. After your third attempt to remind her to call someone to fix your temperamental heater, do you:

A Alert the housing agent to complain about the concierge who should be retired from the position.

B Tell her you have been waiting patiently but it's getting ridiculous having to remind her for the third time.

C Do it yourself. Call the repairman the next day and charge the housing agent.

D Ask the concierge for the number and call the repairman yourself.

Answer

A friend of ours actually lived through this problem and her answer was vehemently *D*. Complaining gets nothing accomplished but breeds bad blood between you and the concierge. If you have to remind her for the third time, there's every likelihood there will be a fourth, and a fifth. The thing not to do is answer *C*, though many take it into their own hands to repair whatever needs repairing. The trouble comes when it is a lousy job done by someone other than the contractor who is supposed to handle all repairs in the building. The responsibility thus falls onto you – and the agency may not want to pay on the pretext that they did not grant you permission to employ someone else.

SCENARIO 7

At the cinema, you encounter a group of noisy teenagers who insist on having a running commentary about the movie. Losing your patience, do you:

A Grit your teeth as you ask them to please keep the noise level down as you are trying to watch the movie.

B Move yourself to another seat.

C Complain to the usher.

D Grin and bear it.

Answer

B. Cowardly as it seems, moving to another seat is the best thing to do since cinemas in Switzerland have a free-seating policy. All the other answers really put one in a foul mood so it's quite self-defeating if all you want to have is a quiet night out at the movies.

SCENARIO 8

The end of your children's school term is two weeks away but the exams are already over. Since your home leave starts a week before school is formally closed, do you:

A Book your flight, pack your bags, and leave.

B Telephone the school and ask for permission to let your children off a week earlier.

C Go personally to the school to request permission to let your children off a week earlier and explain why.

D Spin a yarn about a death in the family and insist on having your children out by a certain date.

Answer

C is the best answer because schools in Switzerland are strict and unless you have a very good reason for taking your children out of

school early, you won't have to book your air ticket early. *A* works if you aren't planning on returning to the same school. *B* is a viable option if you can't make it there personally. *D* is just, well, dishonest.

CHECKLIST FOR THE DEAR DEPARTING

You have approximately six months left before you and your family return to your home country. As you run down the checklist of things to do, which ones do you tick for 'yes', and which ones for 'no'?

1. Alert the commune administration for foreigners that you are leaving the country and return your permit of residency.
2. Start to terminate all contracts with the PTT for the telephone, television, radio and electricity, and put in writing when you will be leaving so as to have your deposits reimbursed on time.
3. Liaise with the apartment-renting agency or landlord when to do an *état-des-lieux* (state of the place check) and when to return the house keys.

4. Go to the PTT to leave your next forwarding address.
5. Look around for freight forwarders if you have a lot of things to ship home.
6. Let the school know that your child/children will be leaving prior to finishing that term.
7. Plan to have a garage sale or call charitable organisations to come by and remove heavy furniture you can't sell.
8. Mend broken furnishings or purchase things that have been broken if your apartment comes furnished.
9. Let your insurance company know you will be terminating all your contracts.
10. Start putting ads into the newspapers if you intend to sell off the car, the furniture, or need to find someone to take over the apartment.
11. Clear all outstanding debts and put a deadline to terminating your bank account(s).

Answer

All of the above should be answered 'yes' three to six months prior to your leaving Switzerland. There have been many cases where there

was not enough time for the authorities to reimburse deposits. In such cases, leave them the bank account number from your home country and ask them to transfer your funds as soon as possible. Have this in writing and always make note of who the person in charge is and when the documents are stamped and dated.

The law-abiding Swiss are law-abiding to the end. If you do not notify them of your departure, bills and other unwanted mail will continue to end up in your mailbox.

GLOSSARY

AHV: Old-age and survivor's insurance.

Canton: Similar to a state or province.

Casco/Casco complet: Types of insurance for your car.

CFF (Chemin de fer Federal): 'Swiss Federal Railways' in French.

CHF (Confédération Helvétique Franc): The monetary unit of Switzerland.

Concierge: The person or persons in charge of maintaining the building.

Contrôle des habitants: The administrative office that handles all the formalities and documents for your residency in Switzerland.

Coop: Large chain supermarket, pronounced Co-Op.

État des lieux: Literally 'the state of the place' – an inspection by the housing agent before you move in and at the end of your lease.

Garantie-loyer: Literally 'the guarantee-rent', two to three months' rent which the housing agent will have you sign for and pay before the keys are given.

La Poste: Post office. (German: Die Post; Italian: La Posta)

Migros: Large chain supermarket. The size of the supermarket is predetermined by the number of M's next to its name. MMM means it is a large Migros supermarket; M means it's a small branch.

Parkomatic: Automatic pay-parking machine.

Permis de circulation: Literally the permit for circulation. This grey leaflet permits the holder to drive the vehicle.

Permis/Genehmigung/Permesso A/B/C: The types of permits Switzerland issues to Foreigners, in French/German/Italian.

RC (Responsabilité civile): Minimum insurance coverage which is mandatory.

Romansch: Language of the people in the Grison area. Also Switzerland's fourth language.

SBB (Schweizerische Bundesbahnen): 'Swiss Federal Railways' in German.

Schweiz/Suisse/Svizzera: 'Switzerland' in German/French/Italian.

Schwyzerdütsch: The Swiss-German dialect.

SNTO: Swiss National Tourist Office.

Standing order: Most banks have this service to automatically pay fixed bills each month like the rent or cable TV.

SUVA: A state-organised compulsory accident insurance programme.

Suisse Romands: The general term for the Swiss-French.

Versement: The green slip you fill up in order to pay your bills via the Post.

Vignette: The highway tax sticker that allows one access onto the freeway. You can purchase *vignettes* at the post office, the frontier posts or the Swiss National Tourist Office.

VF (Version Française): The 'dubbed version'. Subtitles are usually in German or Italian.

VO (Version Originale): This is what you look out for at the movies if the original version is what you want to see.

BIBLIOGRAPHY

Barber, Peter and curators of the British Library and the British Museum. *Switzerland 700* . The British Library: 1991.

Hauser, Albert. *A short history of Swiss industry*. Zollikon, Switzerland: Bosch, 1949.

Honan, Mark. *Switzerland – a travel survival kit*. Lonely Planet Publications, 1994.

Kane, Robert S. *Switzerland at its best*. Passport Books (Tour Guide), 1987.

Krippendorf, Jost. *Tourism in Twentieth Century Switzerland*. California: Society of the Promotion of Science and Scholarship, 1978.

Kummerly + Frey, *Switzerland 1998/1999*.

Landes, David S. *Revolution in Time: Clocks and the Making of the Modern World*. Cambridge, Massachusetts; London: Belknap Press of Harvard University Press, 1983.

Le tourisme suisse en chiffres, edition 1988.

Popular Customs and Festivals in Switzerland. Zurich: Pro Helvetia, 1986.

Suisse Insolite. Editions Mondo, SA. Lausanne, 1970.

Switzerland 1993: People, State, Economy, Culture. Published annually; Bern: Kummerly & Frey.

Switzerland: An inside view. Coordinating Committee for the Presence of Switzerland Abroad (Zurich), 1992.

Widmer, Peter. *Culinary excursions through Switzerland*. Germany: Sigloch Edition, 1985/88.

Wildblood, Richard. *What makes Switzerland unique?* The Book Guild Ltd, 1990.

Recommended Reading

Adler, Florian (editor). *Architectural Guide, Switzerland*. Hans Girsberger, Olinde Riege, Zurich: Artemis, 1978.

Blanc, Emile and Eugène Egger. *Educational Innovations in Switzerland: Traits and Trends*. Paris: Unesco, 1978.

Brookner, Anita. *Hotel du Lac*. Butler & Tanner Ltd, Frome and London, 1984.

Epstein, Eugene V. *Once Upon An Alp*. Zurich: Freiburg, FRG: Atlantis, 1968.

Geissbühler, Karl D. (editor). *Swiss Graphic Design and Photography '82/83*. Zurich Graphic Design and Photography, 1982.

Hahnloser-Ingold, Margrit. *Pandemonium – Jean Tinguely*. Zurich Ex Libris/Kunstkreis; Bern: Benteli, 1988.

Hauser, Albert. *A Short History of Swiss Industry*. Switzerland: Bosch, 1949.

Hildbrand, René (translated by Birgit Rommel). *Tell me a Swiss Joke! Humour from Switzerland. Believe it or not, it exists!* Benteli, Bern, 1987.

Lloyd, Jr., William Bross. *Waging Peace: the Swiss Experience*. Westport, Connecticut: Greenwood, 1980.

Mikes, George. *Switzerland for Beginners*. André Deutsch, 1975.

Müller-Guggenbühl, Fritz. *Swiss Alpine folktales*. London: Oxford University Press, 1958.

Swiss Hotel Association (SHA). *Swiss Hotel Guide*. Swiss Hotel Association, Bern, 1989.

ACKNOWLEDGEMENTS

As Christians living in a Protestant canton, religion did not take precedence over God. We are indeed indebted to God and to the small Bible study group called the International Fellowsheep for giving us the opportunity to put into practice the commandment 'Love your neighbour as yourself.' All Saints' Church in Vevey wasn't our last resort to finding a church home. Curiously enough, miracles work more potently when we realise the futility of relying on oneself.

To the past chaplain David Ritchie and his wife Elisabeth and to the present chaplain Derek Frank and his wife Françoise, we owe a debt of thanks. And if Brian Crook ever gets his hands on a copy of this book somewhere deep in mainland China, I want to say thanks for writing that fateful invitation to us back in May 1992.

To Shirley Hew, friend and fiendish adviser, who thought my being idle was probably criminal and who gave me this superb opportunity to write a *Culture Shock* guide: thanks for going out on a limb and taking me with you! After all, that's where the fruit is.

A special word of thanks to the masterful Monsieur Jean-Jacques Sempé, who inspired me to illustrate in the tradition of *Le Petit Nicholas*.

Grateful thanks to the Swiss Embassy in Singapore for checking the proofs and for many helpful comments.

To Vreni Naess: Thank you for sending me the e-mail back in August 1998, the list of helpful corrections and your ensuing friendship for the past year.

To my little boy with the big heart: Thank you Myron, for letting mama work while you played quietly with your lego, even though you'd rather be wreaking havoc in my studio with your dinosaurs.

Lastly, to my dad. Thank you for giving me the freedom I thought I lacked.

THE AUTHOR

Shirley Eu holds a BFA in advertising/illustration from the Art Center College of Design in Pasadena, USA. She has been art directing, writing and illustrating for different agencies since the first publication of *Culture Shock! Switzerland*. A spirited freelancer by nature, she now lives in Singapore with her young son. Her next few projects include *driting*, a new format of storytelling interspersed with detailed illustrations, holding a one-person exhibition on multi-layered woodcut printing and scrapbook editing her numerous travel tales.

INDEX

Ansermet, Ernest 62
Ammann, Othmar 27
art and culture 58–64
authors, Swiss 60–2

ballet 64
baptism 90
Barth, Karl 30
Basler Leckerli 122
Bern 112
Bernina Hotel 116
Bex 106
bicycling 76
Bill, Max 59
boating 74, 106
breads 117
Brunner, Emil 30
Bullinger, Heinrich 30
Byron, Lord George Gordon 28

Calvin, Jean 29–30
cantons 16–17, 24
car: rental 12, 143
   registration 45
   road tax 45
   driving 93
carnivals 56
Cendrars, Blaise 61
cheeses 117–18
churches 30
CHF 53

climate 35–7
Coop 27, 50, 120
concierge 39, 91
controller of foreigners 24
curling 71
currency 53

Dürrenmatt, Friedrich 61

economy 25–8
education 79–88
Eidgenossenschaft 16
equestrian circuits 75
Escoffier, Auguste 115
Evian 106–7

fairs, national 133
Farel, Guillaume 30
fax 40, 43
Festspiel 63
fondue 125
food 113–26
   recipes 123–6
foodstuff, dried 91
Frisch, Max Rudolf 61
funeral 90

garantie-loyer 38
greetings 96
Grütli 16
gymnasium 82–3

hiking 71, 73
hitching rides 97
Honegger, Arthur 63
hot-air ballooning 71

insurance 43–4, 132–3
immigration 38
ISC symposium 136–8

jazz festivals 64–7

kindergarten 81
Klee, Paul 59
Kunsthaus 60

language 18–23, 101
    French, German ,Italian 20–3
    business 135
Le Corbusier 106, 136
Liechtenstein 109–10
Lugano 110–11
Lyon 108

MAMCO 59
Mammouth 107
markets, farmers' 94, 120
meats 119
Meyer, Conrad-Ferdinand 61
Milan 111–12
minigolf 75
Migros 27, 50, 120
Migros Klubschule 88
Mövenpick 115
movies 49, 64
müesli 116
museums 49, 59–60, 91, 112
music 62–3, 64–6

neighbours 97
Nietzsche, Friedrich 78
Nestlé 27
newspaper kiosks 57
Nytlä 115

Oktoberfest 108–9

parashooting 75
parking fines 98–9
People's Initiative 32–3
permits 24–5, 37–8
Pestalozzi, Johann Heinrich 82
Peter, Daniel 115–16
politics 31–3
potatoes 121
PTT 13, 39, 42–3, 45, 48, 53, 99,
    100, 143
public holidays 49

Ramuz, Charles-Ferdinand 61
recession 48
recycling 53–4, 100
referendum 33
Reformation 82
religion 29–31
Ritz, Cesar 87, 115, 118
rösti 113, 126
Rousseau, Jean-Jacques 55, 61, 82

safety 47–8
Schiller, Friedrich 63
schools *see* education
    private 85–6
Schweizerisches Landesmuseum
    58
schwinging 56, 63
Schwyzerdütsch 18

shopping 50–2
  grocery 96–7
  across borders 97
skiing 69–70
skikjöring 71
sledding 70
snowboarding 70–1
social niceties 20–1
springs, hot 78
summer sports 72–6
Swatch 56
swearing 100
swimming 73–4

taxis 13
telephone 39–40
television 41–2
tennis 76
Tinguely, Jean 58
tipping 100
tobogganing 70
Touring Club of Switzerland 46,
  142
trade, foreign 128
trains 12, 101, 133
transportation 46–7
truancy 80

unemployment 48, 129
university 83–5

vandalism 48, 99
vignette 45
visa 37
voting 32–3

wages 130
weddings 101–3

wines 118–19
winter sports 69–72
work ethics 134
working hours 131–2
World Health Organisation 76,
  101

Zwingli, Ulrich 29